Principles
in Practice

The Principles in Practice imprint offers teachers concrete illustrations of effective classroom practices based in NCTE research briefs and policy statements. Each book discusses the research on a specific topic, links the research to an NCTE brief or policy statement, and then demonstrates how those principles come alive in practice: by showcasing actual classroom practices that demonstrate the policies in action; by talking about research in practical, teacher-friendly language; and by offering teachers possibilities for rethinking their own practices in light of the ideas presented in the books. Books within the imprint are grouped in strands, each strand focused on a significant topic of interest.

Doing and Making Authentic Literacies (2014) Linda Denstaedt, Laura Jane Roop, and
   Stephen Best

Reading in Today's Classrooms Strand

Connected Reading: Teaching Adolescent Readers in a Digital World (2015) Kristen Hawley Turner
   and Troy Hicks
Digital Reading: What's Essential in Grades 3–8 (2015) William L. Bass II and Franki Sibberson
Teaching Reading with YA Literature: Complex Texts, Complex Lives (2016) Jennifer Buehler

Teaching English Language Learners Strand

*Beyond "Teaching to the Test": Rethinking Accountability and Assessment for English Language
   Learners* (2017) Betsy Gilliland and Shannon Pella
Community Literacies en Confianza: *Learning from Bilingual After-School Programs* (2017)
   Steven Alvarez
Understanding Language: Supporting ELL Students in Responsive ELA Classrooms (2017)
   Melinda J. McBee Orzulak
*Writing across Culture and Language: Inclusive Strategies for Working with ELL Writers in the
   ELA Classroom* (2017) Christina Ortmeier-Hooper

Students' Rights to Read and Write Strand

Adventurous Thinking: Fostering Students' Rights to Read and Write in Secondary ELA Classrooms
   (2019) Mollie V. Blackburn, editor
In the Pursuit of Justice: Students' Rights to Read and Write in Elementary School (2020) Mariana
   Souto-Manning, editor
*Already Readers and Writers: Honoring Students' Rights to Read and Write in the Middle Grade
   Classroom* (2020) Jennifer Ochoa, editor

Children's and YA Literature Strand

*Challenging Traditional Classroom Spaces with YA Literature: Students in Community as Course
   Co-Designers* (2022) Ricki Ginsberg
Restorying Young Adult Literature: Expanding Students' Perspectives with Digital Texts (2023)
   James Joshua Coleman, Autumn A. Griffin, and Ebony Elizabeth Thomas

Technology in the Classroom Strand

Reimagining Literacies in the Digital Age: Multimodal Strategies to Teach with Technology (2022)
   Pauline S. Schmidt and Matthew J. Kruger-Ross
Literacies Before Technologies: Making Digital Tools Matter for Middle Grades Learners (2023) Troy
   Hicks and Jill Runstrom

Cultivating Young Multilingual Writers

Nurturing Voices and Stories in and beyond the Classroom Walls

Tracey T. Flores
The University of Texas at Austin

María E. Fránquiz
The University of Texas at Austin

National Council of
Teachers of English

340 N. Neil St., Suite #104, Champaign, Illinois 61820
www.ncte.org

Staff Editor: Cynthia Gomez
Imprint Editor: Cathy Fleischer
Interior Design: Victoria Pohlmann
Cover Design: Pat Mayer
Cover Images: iStock.com/PeopleImages

ISBN 978-0-8141-0152-0 (paperback); 978-0-8141-0153-7 (EPUB); 978-0-8141-0154-4 (PDF)

Library of Congress Control Number: 2023940949

For Milagros, always remember the power of your voice.
For my mom and dad, Vivian and George Flores,
thank you for always encouraging me as a writer.
—TTF

In memory of my parents, Herminio and Esther Fránquiz,
who were my first teachers and gave me a strong
foundation en la fe, la confianza, y la educación.
—MF

Dear Reader,

As a former high school teacher, I remember the frustration I felt when the gap between Research (and that is how I always thought of it: Research with a capital R) and my own practice seemed too wide to ever cross. So many research studies were easy to ignore, in part because they were so distant from my practice and in part because I had no one to help me see how that research would make sense in my everyday practice.

That gap informs the thinking behind this book imprint. Designed for busy teachers, Principles in Practice publishes books that look carefully at NCTE's research reports and policy statements and puts those policies to the test in actual classrooms. The goal: to familiarize teachers with important teaching issues, the research behind those issues, potential resources, and—most of all—make the research and policies come alive for teacher-readers.

This book is part of the strand that focuses on Writing in Today's Classrooms. Each book in the series highlights a different aspect of this important topic and is organized in a similar way: immersing you in the research principles surrounding the topic (as laid out in the NCTE position statement, *Professional Knowledge for the Teaching of Writing*) and then taking you into actual classrooms, teacher discussions, and student work to see how the principles play out. Each book closes with a teacher-friendly bibliography to offer you even more resources.

Good teaching is connected to strong research. We hope these books help you continue the good teaching that you're doing, think hard about ways to adapt and adjust your practice, and grow even stronger and more confident in the vital work you do with kids every day.

Best of luck,

Cathy Fleischer
Imprint Editor

Contents

Acknowledgments

Writing a book is hard. Writing a book during a pandemic is even harder. Schools closed when the world shut down, and we learned new ways to (re)connect, share our challenges, and maintain our humor. Sitting at kitchen tables or office desks, we made connections with the teachers whose voices are part of this book. These connections made the work and world feel a little lighter.

Writing this book took us on many journeys. We journeyed back to our childhoods to remember the practices and pedagogies of our families and the teachers that supported us, in and out of the classroom. We traveled into our own classrooms, where we created learning communities alongside our students to reflect on our own values and beliefs as educators and teacher educators. Writing this book was also a journey into the cultural worlds co-constructed by teachers and students in and through the languages and literacies brought into and valued in their classrooms. In all the journeys, persons, spaces, materials, activities, sharing, and feedback affirmed writers and their developing craft.

Thank you to the talented and fierce teachers and their remarkable students, the heart of this book, for opening your classrooms and lives to us, and now, the world. Thank you for the visits, the phone calls, the Zoom pláticas, and the emails, and for trusting us with your stories. Your voices reverberate throughout each page of this book, your students' writing touches the lives of others, and your teaching will continue to change lives.

Finally, thank you to our editor, Cathy Fleischer, for your patience, guidance, and care along our journey.

Professional Knowledge for the Teaching of Writing

Date: February 28, 2016
Category: 21st Century Literacies, Writing

Approved in February 2016, this revised statement replaces the NCTE Beliefs about the Teaching of Writing (November 2004), now sunsetted.

A subcommittee of the NCTE Executive Committee wrote the *NCTE Beliefs about the Teaching of Writing* in 2004. In over a decade since, the everyday experience of writing in people's lives has expanded dramatically. Increasingly, handheld devices are important instruments for people's writing, integrated tightly, nearly seamlessly, with their composing in video, photographs, and other media. Geographic location and embodied presence have become more salient to writing than at most times in human history. The ways writing and the spoken voice are mutually supportive in writing processes have become increasingly facilitated by technological capabilities. Globalized economies and relative ease of transportation have continued to bring languages into contact with one another, and US educational scholars and, sometimes, institutions have made progress in considering what it means for individuals to be adding new written languages to existing ones. Even as these expansions have enlarged the experience of writing outside school, implementation of the first USA nationwide standards in literacy—the Common Core State Standards—has, in some places, contributed to narrowing students' experience of writing inside school. In that contradictory and shifting environment, the NCTE Executive Committee charged a committee to update the *Beliefs about the Teaching of Writing*, attempting to reflect some of the historically significant changes of recent years. What follows are ten of the professional principles that guide effective teaching of writing. Each principle is followed by an explanation of what the principle means for teaching and where teachers can find related content in NCTE statements.

Writing grows out of many purposes.

Writing is not just one practice or activity. A note to a cousin is not like a business report, which is different again from a poem. The processes and ways of thinking that lead to these varied kinds of texts can also vary widely, from the quick email to a friend to the careful drafting and redrafting of a legal contract. The different purposes and genres both grow out of and create varied relationships between the writers and the readers, and existing relationships are reflected in degrees of formality in language, as well as assumptions about what knowledge and experience are already shared, and what needs to be explained. Writing with certain purposes in mind, the writer focuses attention on what the audience is thinking or believing; other times, the writer focuses more on the information she or he is organizing, or on her or his own emergent thoughts and feelings. Therefore, the thinking, procedures, and physical format in writing are shaped in accord with the author's purpose(s), the needs of the audience, and the conventions of the genre.

Often, in school, students write only to prove that they did something they were asked to do, in order to get credit for it. Or, students are taught a single type of writing and are led to believe this type will suffice in all situations. Since writers outside school have many different purposes beyond demonstrating accountability and they use more diverse genres of writing, it is important that students have experiences within school that teach them how writing differs with purpose, audience, and other elements of the situation. Even within more academic settings like college courses, the characteristics of good writing vary among disciplines; what counts as a successful lab report, for example, differs from a successful history paper, online discussion contribution, essay exam, reflection on service learning, or interpretative statement about a work of art.

Thus, beyond the traditional purposes that are identified in school, purposes for writing include developing social networks; reasoning with others to improve society; supporting personal and spiritual growth; reflecting on experience; communicating professionally and academically; building relationships with others, including friends, family, and like-minded individuals; and engaging in aesthetic experiences.

What does this mean for teaching?

In order to provide high-quality writing opportunities for all students, teachers need to understand:

- The wide range of purposes for which people write and the different kinds of texts and processes that arise from those purposes;
- Strategies and forms for writing for public participation in a democratic society;
- Ways people use writing for personal growth, expression, and reflection, and how to encourage and develop this kind of writing;
- How people make creative and literary texts, aesthetic genres, for the purposes of entertainment, pleasure, or exploration;
- The ways digital environments have added new modalities while constantly creating new publics, audiences, purposes, and invitations to compose;
- The range of non-public uses of writing for self-organization, reflection, planning, and management of information, and the many tools, digital and otherwise, that people use for these purposes;
- Appropriate genres for varied academic disciplines and the purposes and relationships that create those forms;
- Ways of organizing and transforming school curricula in order to provide students with adequate education in varied purposes for writing; and
- How to set up a course that asks students to write for varied purposes and audiences.

Related:

Writing Now: A Policy Research Brief Produced by the National Council of Teachers of English

Writing is embedded in complex social relationships and their appropriate languages.

Writing happens in the midst of a web of relationships. Most clearly, the relationship between the writer and the reader can be very specific: writers often have a definite idea of who will read their work, not just a generalized notion that their text will be available to the world. Furthermore, particular people surround the writer—other writers, friends, members of a given community— during the process of composing. They may know what the writer is doing and be indirectly involved in it, though they are not the audience for the work. In workplace and academic settings, writers often write because someone in authority tells them to. Therefore, power relationships are built into the writing situation. In every writing situation, the writer, the reader, and all relevant others live in a structured social order, where some people's words count more than others, where being heard is more difficult for some people than others, where some people's words come true and others' do not.

Writers start in different places. It makes a difference what kinds of language writers spoke while growing up and may speak at home now, and how those experiences relate to the kinds of language they are being asked to take when composing. It makes a difference, too, the culture a writer comes from, the ways people use language in that culture and the degree to which that culture is privileged in the larger society. Important cultural differences are not only linguistic but also racial, economic, geographic, and ideological. Digital environments have created new contexts in which new languages are being invented continuously, and young people are often leading innovators of "digitalk." The internet brings global languages into contact, even as it provides new contexts for each language—written and oral—to change.

What does this mean for teaching?

The teaching of writing should assume students will begin with the language with which they are most at home and most fluent in their speech. That language may be a variety of English or a different language altogether. The languages students learn first are the bedrock upon which all other language traditions and forms will be constructed. The ultimate goal is not to leave students where they are, however, but to move them toward greater flexibility, so that they can write not just for their own intimates but for wider audiences. Teachers will want to engage in respectful inquiry with students about significant differences between patterns in their use of their first language and more conventionally written English. Even as they move toward more widely used English, writers find that it is not necessary or desirable to eliminate the ways their family and people in their neighborhood use words to express themselves. The teaching of excellence in writing means adding language to what already exists, not subtracting. Further, expert writing teachers deliberately teach students to incorporate their heritage and home languages intentionally and strategically in the texts they write. The goal is to make more relationships available, not fewer.

In order to provide high-quality writing opportunities for all students, teachers need to understand:

- How to find out about students' language use in the home and their neighborhoods, the changes in language context they may have encountered in their lives, and the kinds of language they most value;
- The ways wider social situations in which students speak, write, read, and relate to other people affect what feels to them natural or unnatural, easy or hard;
- How mixing languages within a text can promote students' acquisition of academic language, deeper competence in a repertoire of codes, ability to communicate complex thoughts, and ways of communicating with various audiences;
- How teachers who do not speak or understand a student's home language can embrace and support the use of home languages in the classroom;
- How to discuss respectfully with students expectations for flexibility in the employment of different kinds of language for different social contexts in order to gain access to some powerful social worlds;

- How to help students negotiate maintenance of their most familiar and cherished language practices while developing strength in academic classroom English;
- Control and awareness of their own varied and strategic ways of using language and the social contexts that expect them;
- An understanding of the relationships among group affiliation, identity, and language;
- Knowledge of the usual patterns of common dialects in English, such as African American English, Spanish, and varieties of English related to Spanish, common patterns in American rural and urban populations, predictable patterns in the English varieties of groups common in their teaching contexts; and
- The online spaces through which students communicate, and how their uses of digitalk differs from conventional written English.

Related:
CCCC Statement on Second Language Writing and Writers
Resolution on the Student's Right to Incorporate Heritage and Home Languages in Writing

Composing occurs in different modalities and technologies.

Composing has always required technology, whether it's the technology we associate with print—including pens, pencils, and paper—or the technology we associate with the digital—including word processors, digital imaging software, and the internet. Like all texts, print texts are multimodal: print, whether hand-created or machine-produced, relies for meaning on multiple modalities, including language, layout, and the visual characteristics of the script. Moreover, print has often included visuals—including maps, line drawings, illustrations, and graphs—to create a fuller representation of meaning, to tap the familiarity of a visual to help readers make meaning in a new genre, to add aesthetic value, and to appeal to a wider audience. Film, television, and video involve such combinations of modalities, as do presentation software and websites. As technologies for composing have expanded, "composing" has increasingly referred to a suite of activities in varied modalities. Composers today work with many modalities, including language, layout, still images, other visuals, video, and sound. Computers, both the stationary and mobile varieties, provide a work environment where composers can employ and combine these modalities. Moreover, the internet not only makes a range of new and diverse materials available to writers, but also brings writers and readers closer together and makes possible new kinds of collaborations. Thus, when students have access to a computer with full internet access, composing opportunities expand.

Additionally, increased access to various modalities and technologies has created opportunities for students with a wide range of abilities, backgrounds, and languages to compose with more independence and agency. As more digital tools become available, and more forms of expression are not only accepted but expected, more students are able to employ these tools independently.

What does this mean for teaching?

Writing instruction should support students as they compose with a variety of modalities and technologies. Because students will, in the wider world, be using word processing for drafting, revision, and editing, incorporating visual components in some compositions, and including links where appropriate, definitions of composing should include these practices; definitions that exclude them are out-of-date and inappropriate.

Because many teachers and students do not have access to the most up-to-date technologies, such as portable devices with cameras, teaching students to compose multimodally may best be accomplished by foregrounding multimodal dimensions of composing in low-tech environments. An assignment for students to create picture books, for example, can allow them to consider how languages and images complement each other and assist the reader. Similar kinds of visual/verbal thinking can be supported across the school curriculum through other illustrated text forms, including journals, design notebooks, and posters. Attention to modalities in assignments and genres like these demonstrates the extent to which "new" literacies are rooted in older ones.

In order to provide high-quality writing opportunities for all students, teachers need to understand:

- A range of new genres that have emerged on the internet;
- Open-source platforms that students can use for composing and electronic portfolios;
- Design and layout principles for print and digital publication;
- Conventions for digital communication, including email, chat, text messages, social networking, and online discussion forums;
- Ways to navigate both the World Wide Web and web-based databases;
- Ways to access, evaluate, use, and cite information found on the internet;
- Theory about and history of modalities, technologies, and the affordances they offer for meaning making;
- Operation of hardware and software that composers use, including resources for solving software and hardware problems;
- Tools that help students compose as independently as possible, in the modalities that best fit their needs and purposes; and
- internet resources for remaining up-to-date on technologies.

Related:
Resolution on Composing with Nonprint Media
Position Statement on Multimodal Literacies
CCCC Position Statement on Teaching, Learning, and Assessing Writing in Digital Environments
21st-Century Literacies: A Policy Research Brief

Conventions of finished and edited texts are an important dimension of the relationship between writers and readers.

Readers expect writing to conform to their expectations. For public texts written for a general audience, contemporary readers expect words to be spelled in a standardized way, for punctuation to be used in predictable ways, for usage and syntax to match that used in texts they already acknowledged as successful. They expect the style in a piece of writing to be appropriate to its genre and social situation. With that in mind, writers try to use these surface elements strategically, in order to present the identity, create the relationships, and express the ideas that suit their purpose.

What does this mean for teaching?
Every teacher has to resolve a tension between writing as generating and shaping ideas and writing as a final product, demonstrating expected surface conventions. On the one hand, it is

important for writing to be as correct as possible and for students to be able to produce correct texts so that readers can read and make meaning from them. On the other hand, achieving correctness is only one set of things writers must be able to do; a correct document empty of ideas or unsuited to its audience or purpose is not a good piece of writing. There is no formula for resolving this tension. Though it may be desirable both fluently to produce writing and to adhere to conventions, growth in fluency and control of conventions may not occur at the same time. If a student's mental energies are focused on new intellectual challenges, he or she may attend less fully to details of grammar and punctuation.

Such uneven development should be tolerated and, in fact, encouraged. Too much emphasis on correctness can actually inhibit a writer's development. By the same token, without mastering conventions for written discourse, writers may find their efforts regarded less highly by readers they had wanted to influence. Each teacher must be knowledgeable enough about the entire landscape of writing instruction to guide particular students toward a goal, including increasing fluency in new contexts, mastering conventions, and perhaps most important, developing rhetorical sophistication and appropriateness—all of which work together. NCTE's stated policy over many years has been that conventions of writing are best taught in the context of writing.

Most writing teachers teach students how to edit their writing that will be shared with audiences. This is often considered a late stage in the process of composing, because editing is only essential for the words, visuals, and other materials that are left after all the cutting, replacing, rewriting, and adding that go on during revision. Writers keep an image in their minds of conventional grammar, spelling, and punctuation in order to compare what is already on the page to what their audience expects. They also need to be aware of stylistic options and larger language choices that will best articulate their ideas and produce the most desirable impression on their readers. Language choices may be a matter of the identity a writer seeks to project, and those identities may not be productively standardized. In digital environments, there may be an expected way of using language due to the nature of the platform, such as in texting or blogging, where the conventional usage might differ from language in other contexts.

An area of consideration with respect to conventions in writing is the development of language proficiency for students learning English as an additional language. Experienced teachers understand that these multilingual students will enter the classroom at different stages and vary in the pace with which they acquire their new language. Knowledge of students' cultural and linguistic background and the way that background intersects or differs from English language conventions helps ensure that students are receiving instruction appropriate for their current stage of language learning. Writers who are learning English as an additional language will have multiple possible patterns in mind for phonology, morphology, syntax, and often genre and pragmatics as well. That is, they know more, and are sorting through that knowledge. Some may require support in analyzing the expectations of a wider English-dominant audience in contrast to the patterns of their earlier language(s). For many, patterns from the first language will persist and should be treated with the respect and generosity that should be afforded to spoken accented English.

In order to provide high-quality writing opportunities for all students, teachers need to understand:

- Developmental factors in writing, including the tension between fluency with new operations or content and the practices that produce accepted spelling, punctuation, syntactic, and usage conventions;

- Diverse influences and constraints on writers' decision making as they determine the conventions that apply to this situation and this piece of writing;
- A variety of applications and options for most conventions;
- Appropriate conventions for writing for a particular public audience;
- Linguistic terminology that is helpful for teaching particular kinds of usage without employing excessive linguistic terminology;
- Linguistic terminology helpful for communicating professionally with other educators;
- The relationship among rhetorical considerations and decisions about conventions, for example, the conditions under which a dash, a comma, a semicolon, or a full stop might be more effective;
- Conventions beyond the sentence, such as effective uses of bulleted lists, mixed genres and voices, diagrams and charts, design of pages, and composition of video shots;
- The conditions under which people learn to participate in new social situations, both personal and professional, with language; and
- How to understand technologies such as grammar and spelling checkers to decide which changes are applicable in a given editing situation.

Related:
Students' Right to Their Own Language
CCCC Statement on Second Language Writers and Writing

Everyone has the capacity to write; writing can be taught; and teachers can help students become better writers.

Developing writers require support. This support can best come through carefully designed writing instruction oriented toward acquiring new strategies and skills. Certainly, writers can benefit from teachers who simply support and give them time to write. However, high-quality instruction matters. Teachers of writing should be well versed in composition theory and research, and they should know methods for turning that theory into practice. They should be capable of teaching writing in both print and digital environments.

Students are different from one another, and they bring to the experience of writing a wide range of resources and strengths. At the same time, any writer can be positioned as weak, struggling, or incompetent. All writers need to learn multiple strategies and modalities to compensate for moments when they feel stuck or defeated, to get on with the business of composing.

As is the case with many activities, becoming a better writer requires that students write. This means actual writing for real audiences, not merely listening to lectures about writing, doing grammar drills, or discussing readings. The more people write, the more familiar it becomes and the more they are motivated to do it. Writers learn from each session with their hands on a keyboard or fingers on a pencil as they draft, rethink, revise, and draft again. Improvement is built into the experience of writing when writers revise, strategizing ways to make their writing better.

What does this mean for teaching?

Writing instruction must include ample in-class and out-of-class opportunities for writing, including writing in digital spaces, and should involve writing for a variety of purposes and audiences, including audiences beyond the classroom. Teachers need to support students in the development of writing lives, habits, and preferences for life outside school. We already know that many students do extensive amounts of self-sponsored writing: emailing, keeping journals or doing creative projects, instant messaging, making websites, blogging, creating fan fiction. Though critically important for college and career, the teaching of writing should also be geared toward making sense in a life outside of school, so that writing has ample room to grow in individuals' lives. It is useful for teachers to consider what elements of their curriculum they could imagine students self-sponsoring outside school. Ultimately, those are the activities that will produce more writing.

In order to provide high-quality writing opportunities for all students, teachers need to understand:

- How to interpret curriculum documents, including standards, skills, strategies, concepts, and content that can be taught while students are actually writing, rather than one dimension of composing at a time to all students at once;
- How to create writing lives for the world beyond school;
- How to construct social structures that support independent work;
- How to confer with individual writers;
- How to assess students' work while they are in the process of writing—formatively—in order to offer timely assistance during the composing process;
- How to plan what students need to know in response to ongoing research;
- How to create a sense of community and personal safety in the classroom, so that students are willing to write and collaborate freely and at length;
- How to effectively employ a variety of technologies such as brainstorming tools, collaborative word processors, and bibliography managers for students to engage in writing fully;
- How to ensure that every student has the tools and supports necessary to be as independent as possible; and
- How to encourage and include students writing in their home languages.

Related:
NCTE Beliefs about Students' Right to Write
Resolution on Students' Right of Expression
What We Know about Writing, Grades K–2
How to Help Your Child Become a Better Writer (English)
How to Help Your Child Become a Better Writer (Español)

Writing is a process.

Often, when people think of writing, they think of texts—finished pieces of writing that stand alone. Understanding what writers do, however, involves both thinking about what texts look like when they are finished as well as thinking about what strategies writers might employ to produce those texts, especially when using a variety of technologies. Knowledge about writing is only complete when writers understand the ensemble of actions in which they engage as they produce texts. Such understanding has two aspects, at least. First is the development, through extended practice over years, of a repertory of routines, skills, strategies, and practices, for generating, revising, and editing different kinds of texts. Second is the development of reflective abilities and meta-awareness about writing. The procedural knowledge developed through reflective practice helps writers most when they encounter difficulty, or when they are in the middle of creating a piece of writing. How does someone get started? What do they do when they get stuck? How do they plan the overall process, each section of their work, and even the rest of the sentence they are writing right now? Research, theory, and practice in the teaching of writing have produced a rich understanding of what writers do, those who are proficient and professional as well as those who struggle.

Two further points are vital. First, to say that writing is a process is decidedly not to say that it should—or can—be turned into a formulaic set of steps or reduced to a set of traits. Experienced writers shift between different operations according to their audience, the purpose of the writing task, the genre, and circumstances, such as deadlines and considerations of length, style, and format.

Second, writers do not accumulate process skills and strategies once and for all. They develop and refine writing skills throughout their writing lives, as they take up new tasks in new genres for new audiences. They grow continually, across personal and professional contexts, using numerous writing spaces and technologies.

What does this mean for teaching?

Whenever possible, teachers should attend to the process that students might follow to produce texts—and not only specify criteria for evaluating finished products, in form or content. Students should become comfortable with prewriting techniques, multiple strategies for developing and organizing a message, a variety of strategies for revising and editing, and methods for preparing products for public audiences and for deadlines. In explaining assignments, teachers should provide guidance and options for ways of accomplishing the objectives. Using formative assessment to understand the processes students follow—the decisions they make, the attempts along the way—can be at least as important as evaluating the final product with a holistic score or grade. Moreover, they should understand how various digital writing tools—mind mapping, word processing, bibliography managers—can be employed in academically useful ways. At least some of the time, the teacher should guide the students through the process, assisting them as they go. Writing instruction must provide opportunities for students to identify the processes that work best for themselves as they move from one initial idea to final draft, from one writing situation to another.

Writing instruction must also take into account that a good deal of workplace writing and other writing takes place in collaborative situations. Writers must learn to work effectively with one another to create writing, provide feedback, and complete a final draft, often with the use of collaborative technologies.

In order to provide high-quality writing opportunities for all students, teachers need to understand:

- The relationship between features of finished writing and the actions writers perform to create that writing;
- What writers of different genres, including political arguments, stories, poems, blog posts, technical reports, and more, say about their craft;
- The process of writing from the inside, that is, what the teachers themselves as writers experience in a host of different writing situations;
- Multiple strategies for approaching a wide range of typical problems writers face during composing, including strategies for invention, audience, and task analysis, incorporation of images and other visuals, revision, and editing;

- Multiple, flexible models of the writing process, the varied ways individuals approach similar tasks, and the ways that writing situations and genres inform processes;
- How to design time and possibly staged intervals of work for students to do their best work on a given assignment; and
- A range of digital writing tools that writers might find useful in their processes, including word processors, databases, outliners, mind mapping software, design software, shared-document websites, and other hardware, software, and web-based technologies.

Related:
Framework for Success in Postsecondary Writing
CCCC Principles for the Postsecondary Teaching of Writing

Writing is a tool for thinking.

When writers actually write, they think of things that they did not have in mind before they began writing. The act of writing generates ideas; writing can be an act of discovery. This is different from the way we often think of writers—as the solitary author who works diligently to get ideas fixed in his or her head before writing them down. The notion that writing is a medium for thought is important in several ways and suggests a number of important uses for writing: to solve problems, to identify issues, to construct questions, to reconsider something one had already figured out, to try out a half-baked idea. This insight that writing is a tool for thinking helps us to understand the process of drafting and revision as one of exploration, and is nothing like the idea of writing as transcribing from prerecorded tape. Nor is the writing process simply fixing the mistakes in an early draft; rather, it involves finding more and more wrinkles and implications in what one is talking about.

What does this mean for teaching?

In any writing classroom, some of the writing is for the writer and some for other audiences as well. Regardless of the age, ability, or experience of the writer, the use of writing to generate thought is still valuable; therefore, forms of writing such as personal narrative, journals, written reflections, observations, and writing-to-learn strategies should be included in the curriculum.

In order to provide high-quality writing opportunities for all students, teachers need to understand:

- How to employ varied tools for thinking through writing, such as journals, writers' notebooks, blogs, sketchbooks, digital portfolios, listservs or online discussion groups, dialogue journals, double-entry or dialectical journals, and others;
- The kinds of new thinking—such as questioning, discovery, and invention—that occur when writers revise;
- The varieties of thinking people do when they compose, and what those types of thinking look like when they appear in writing;
- Strategies for getting started with an idea, or finding an idea when one does not occur immediately;
- Exploring various technologies such as drawing tools and voice-to-text translators for brainstorming and developing one's initial thinking; and

- Ways to accommodate differences among students, such as those who find writing physically challenging, by using oral rehearsal of ideas, gesture, diagramming, or other options that would still allow exploration and development of thought.

Related:
Resolution on Writing Across the Curriculum

Writing has a complex relationship to talk.

From its beginnings in early childhood, through K–12 and college classrooms, and throughout a variety of workplaces and community settings, writing exists in an environment of talk. Speakers often write notes or scripts. Writers often talk in order to rehearse the language and content that will go into what they write, and conversation often provides an impetus or occasion for writing. Writers sometimes confer with teachers and other writers about what to do next, how to improve their drafts, or how to clarify their ideas and purposes. Their usual ways of speaking either may or may not feed into the sentences they write, depending on intricate, continuous, important decisions.

What does this mean for teaching?

In early childhood, teachers expect lots of talk to surround writing, since children are figuring out how to get speech onto paper. Early teaching in composition should also attend to helping children get used to producing language orally, through telling stories, explaining how things work, predicting what will happen, and guessing about why things and people are the way they are. Early writing experiences will often include students explaining orally what is in a text, whether it is printed or drawn.

As they grow, writers still need opportunities to talk about what they are writing about, to rehearse the language of their upcoming texts and run ideas by trusted colleagues before and as they take the risk of committing words to paper. After making a draft, it is often helpful for writers to discuss with peers what they have done, partly in order to get ideas from their peers, partly to see what they, the writers, say when they try to explain their thinking. Writing conferences, wherein student writers talk about their work with a teacher, who can make suggestions or reorient what the writer is doing, are also very helpful uses of talk in the writing process.

In order to provide high-quality writing opportunities for all students, teachers need to understand:

- Ways of setting up and managing student talk in partnerships and groups;
- Ways of establishing a balance between talk and writing in classroom management;
- Ways of organizing the classroom and/or schedule to permit individual teacher-student conferences;
- Strategies for deliberate insertions of opportunities for talk into the writing process: knowing when and how students should talk about their writing;
- Ways of anticipating and solving interpersonal conflicts that arise when students discuss writing;
- Relationships—both similarities and differences—between oral and literate language;
- The uses of writing in public presentations and the values of students making oral presentations that grow out of and use their writing; and

• How technologies such as voice recording apps on smartphones and audio editing tools can be used as students create podcasts, videos, or other multimedia work in which they share their writing through oral production.

Related:
What We Know about Writing, Grades 3–5
What We Know about Writing, Grades 6–8

Writing and reading are related.

Writing and reading are related. People who engage in considerable reading often find writing an easier task, though the primary way a writer improves is through writing. Still, it's self-evident that to write a particular kind of text, it helps if the writer has read that kind of text, if only because the writer then has a mental model of the genre. In order to take on a particular style of language, it also helps to have read that language, to have heard it in one's mind, so that one can hear it again in order to compose it.

Writing can also help people become better readers. In their earliest writing experiences, children listen for the relationships of sounds to letters, which contributes greatly to their phonemic awareness and phonics knowledge. Writers also must learn how texts are structured, because eventually they have to compose in different genres, and that knowledge of structure helps them to predict and make sense of the sections and sequencing of the texts they read. The experience of plotting a short story, organizing a research report, or making line breaks in a poem permits the writer, as a reader, to approach new reading experiences with more informed eyes.

Additionally, reading is a vital source of information and ideas. For writers fully to contribute to a given topic or to be effective in a given situation, they must be familiar with and draw on what previous writers have said. Reading also creates a sense of what one's audience knows or expects on a topic.

What does this mean for teaching?

One way teachers help students become better writers is to make sure they have lots of extended time to read, in school and out. Teachers also make sure students have access to and experience in reading material that presents both professionally published and student writing in various genres. If one is going to write in a genre, it is very helpful to have read in that genre first.

Overall, frequent conversations about the connections between what we read and what we write are helpful. These connections will sometimes be about the structure and craft of the writing itself, and sometimes about thematic and content connections.

In order to provide high-quality writing opportunities for all students, teachers need to understand:

• How writers read for the purposes of writing—with an eye toward not just what the text says but also how it is put together;

• The psychological and social processes reading and writing have in common;

• The ways writers imagine their intended readers, anticipating their responses and needs;

• That text structures are fluid enough to accommodate frequent exceptions, innovations, and disruptions; and

• How writers can identify mentor or exemplar texts, both print and digital, that they may want to emulate in their own writing.

Related:
On Reading, Learning to Read, and Effective Reading Instruction
Reading and Writing across the Curriculum: A Policy Research Brief
Framework for Success in Postsecondary Writing

Assessment of writing involves complex, informed, human judgment.

Assessment of writing occurs for different purposes. The most fundamental and important assessment of writing is that of the writer, whose efficacy and growth demands that she or he determine and intend what to work on next, throughout the process of producing a single text and across experiences as she or he grows through a writing life. Sometimes, a teacher assesses in order to decide what the student has achieved and what he or she still needs to learn. Sometimes, an agency or institution beyond the classroom assesses a student's level of achievement in order to say whether he or she can go on to some new educational level that requires the writer to be able to do certain things. At other times, school authorities require a writing test as a mechanism for requiring teachers to teach writing, or a certain kind or genre of writing. Still other times, as in a history or literature exam, the assessment of writing itself is not the point, but the quality of the writing is evaluated almost in passing.

In any of these assessments of writing, complex judgments are required. Human beings need to make these judgments, not software programmed to score essays, because only human beings can be sensitive enough to purposes, audience, quality and relevance of evidence, truth in content, and the like. Furthermore, such judgments should be made by professionals who are educated and informed about writing, writing development, the various ways writing can be assessed, and the ways such assessments can support writers.

Instructors of composition should know about various methods of assessment of student writing. Instructors must recognize the difference between formative and summative evaluation and be prepared to evaluate students' writing from both perspectives. By formative evaluation here, we mean provisional, ongoing, in-process judgments about what students know and what to teach next—assessments that may be complex descriptions and not reduced to a grade or score and that are intended to support students' writerly development. By summative evaluation, we mean final judgments about the quality of student work (typically reflected in a grade).

In order to provide high-quality writing opportunities for all students, teachers need to understand:

- How to find out what student writers can do, informally, on an ongoing basis;
- How to use that assessment in order to decide what and how to teach next;
- How to assess occasionally, less frequently, in order to form and report judgments about the quality of student writing and learning;
- How to assess ability and knowledge across multiple different writing engagements;
- What the features of good writing are, appropriate to the context and purposes of the teaching and learning;
- What the elements of a constructive process of writing are, appropriate to the context and purposes of the teaching and learning;
- What growth in writing looks like, the developmental aspects of writing ability;
- Ways of assessing student metacognitive process as they connect writing to reading;

- How to recognize in student writing (in both their texts and their actions) the nascent potential for excellence at the features and processes desired;

- How to deliver useful feedback, appropriate for the writer and the situation;

- How to analyze writing situations for their most essential elements, so that assessment is not of everything about writing all at once, but rather is targeted to outcomes;

- How to analyze and interpret both qualitative and quantitative writing assessments and make decisions about their usefulness;

- How to evaluate electronic texts;

- How to use portfolios to assist writers in their development and how to assess portfolios;

- How self-assessment and reflection contribute to a writer's development and ability to move among genres, media, and rhetorical situations; and

- How to employ a variety of technologies—including screencasting and annotation, embedded text and voice comments, and learning management systems—to provide timely, useful, and goal-oriented feedback to students.

Related:
Writing Assessment: A Position Statement of CCCC
NCTE Position Statement on Machine Scoring
NCTE Resolution on Grading Student Writing

Young Multilingual Writers Writing in and beyond the Classroom Walls

Chapter One

My Mexican Culture

I've lived in America my whole life but still embrace some of my Mexican culture like my language, which is something that is very important to me. Somehow, it makes me feel special because when I think of my family, I think of México or even the language Spanish and that is why México and the language Spanish are special to me. Spanish reminds me of my family and culture, which makes me feel strong and powerful.

Something else that reminds me of my Mexican culture is food. Some types of food that remind me of my family and my culture are quesadillas, tamales, and barbacoa. The real reason these foods are special to me is that I get to share them with my family. They remind me of a part of my culture that I don't show very much.

Another thing that I love about my Mexican culture is the stories that my family tells me. My whole mom's side of the family is Mexican, so they tell me stories about their childhood and how they grew up so much differently than me. The stories are always so amazing. They are like windows that let me see into their life and how interesting it is.

*V*irginia, a fourth-grade writer from Austin, Texas, wrote a piece titled "My Mexican Culture." In her writing, Virginia describes the strength and power she feels as both an American and Mexican, embracing language, food, and stories as important parts of her identity and culture. Her words celebrate the beauty of her heritage and also reveal a deep connection to her family and their history. In Virginia's writing, she shares the beauty of being Mexican American while using her voice to "change people's minds" about Mexicans so that everyone can be seen, heard, and treated with respect. This type of bicultural voice (Darder, 2012) has been noted in studies in language arts classrooms as an important element for expanding identities and repertoires (Fránquiz & Salazar, 2004). In a bicultural orientation, the changing of minds that Virginia mentions brings visibility to the struggle of claiming hyphenated and multicultural identities when biased societal structures toward the children of immigrants from México (Darder, 1991; Rumbaut, 2005) and other children from Communities of Color exist.

Contextualizing Writing

Virginia attends a K–5 school located in Central Texas. This school is situated in the middle of an economically and demographically changing neighborhood, in which recently flipped houses, newly built condos and townhomes, and Section Eight housing back up to the fence surrounding the school playground. Even though there are major shifts in the neighborhood as gentrification spreads, the school community remains consistent, strong, and vibrant in its anti-bias curriculum.

Virginia is enrolled in a dual-language (DL) classroom, where she receives instruction throughout the school day in English and Spanish. Her classroom experiences provide her with access to a curriculum delivered in her home and community languages. This supports her in further developing and sustaining her Spanish language, which she describes, in her writing, as deeply connected to her cultural identity.

She wrote this piece as part of a larger writing unit of study focused on identity. Her teacher, Ms. Soledad Bautista, designed this unit to open space for her students to examine and author their identities in writing. Ms. Bautista was invested in all classroom members exploring and noting their unique perspectives and experiences.

For five weeks, she and her young writers gathered ideas and discussed them with partners, during individual conferences, and as a community. As a member of the classroom community, Ms. Bautista shared her own writing and thinking, which opened up a lens into her life and what was important and mattered to her. They read different intentionally selected mentor texts, engaging in rich dialogue about purpose, audience, and authors' craft. Each writer then selected an idea to take through the writing process toward publication. They further explored their topics by reading more mentor texts directly related to their selected topics and tried on different strategies in their writing.

Every writer in Ms. Bautista's community chose to write about a topic that was both personal and unique to their lived realities. Like Virginia, some writers wrote about their cultures, while others wrote about human rights, racism, or their families' (im)migration stories. Each writer took their ideas through the writing process, learning a variety of revising and editing strategies, to support them in publication. Although some writers chose to write about similar experiences, their unique perspectives and voices were evident in their approaches and their final, polished pieces. Their words and stories are situated within the local and global context in which they live, play, and learn—and their writings serve particular purposes within their community and sociocultural world (Rogoff, 1990; Vygotsky, 1987; Wertsch, 1998). As an example, Virginia expressed that her heritage land, México, and her membership to the Mexican American community ought to be respected, honored, and preserved by her own community as well as by the larger cultural world outside her community.

Ms. Bautista explains that the purposes for writing process practices in her classroom embody her goals for students as writers and human beings. She believes in "teaching children that they matter, that they are citizens of the world, and that they have a right to have an opinion about it and the right to say it loud."

Showcasing Writing

At the end of the unit, Ms. Bautista and the entire fourth-grade team invited families and the school community to a celebration of their writing. Invitations were designed, food was prepared, and the cafeteria was transformed into a community art and writing gallery. On the night of the celebration, parents, siblings, neighbors, teachers, and school administration strolled through a gallery of original art and writing composed by the young writers, giving them a real audience for their work. This public display of writing provided each young writer with the opportunity to see the power of their bilingual voices and bicultural stories beyond the classroom walls.

Ms. Bautista's practice is rooted in her belief that writing is the most valuable tool for students to develop and amplify their own voices. She is inspired by the way that she learned how to write, which she describes as a process of deep reflection and examination of thinking about herself and the world. Her beliefs and her own experiences as a writer have influenced her practice as she is always "looking to what will be the most embracing way to develop student's voice and identity as their most valuable resources."

Here, we see how Ms. Bautista puts her theories about writing and developing writers into practice. We see how her students use writing as tools to examine their lived experiences. These young writers understand the power of their voices and perspectives, and how their writing can educate people and share the ideas that are most important in their lives. In their compositions, these young writers are taking risks by sharing a part of themselves with their peers, their teacher, and their families and community. This type of writing takes time to nurture and develop. It happens within a community where young writers are encouraged and supported in taking brave steps as composers, amplifying their voices in the world.

Culture and identity plays a role in the writing - relationships before rigor

Writing in community and writing bravely begins with our own beliefs as teachers of young writers. It is a deep belief that we, as authors of this book, value and hold—a belief that drives our own work alongside young writers and their teachers, and that drives our work in preparing literacy educators and researchers. More important, it is a belief recognized in the NCTE position statement on *Professional Knowledge for the Teaching of Writing* (2016). As articulated in the statement, we believe that, "Everyone has the capacity to write; writing can be taught; and teachers can help students become better writers" (*Professional Knowledge*, 2016). This perspective on writing challenges teachers to interrogate their own beliefs and assumptions about their writers and the teaching of writing, and how they design instruction that tends to the strengths, resources, and needs of each writer in their learning communities.

Everyone Has the Capacity to Write

The belief that everyone has the capacity to write suggests that to grow writers, we must start *with* the writer. As teachers of young writers, we need to recognize that our "writers start in different places" (*Professional Knowledge*, 2016) and sometimes in different languages. Each of our young writers comes to our learning communities with their own history and relationship to writing. They may have experienced success or failure related to writing in general or a genre in particular. Maybe they have never truly had a teacher who saw their capacity as a writer or provided them with quality writing instruction. It's also possible that in their previous classrooms, writing was not viewed as a content area, but through a prescriptive lens and frame detached from their linguistic and cultural experiences in their homes and communities. Young writers' histories and stories and relationship to writing matter deeply and can be expanded whether former instruction was thin or thick.

Writing Can Be Taught and Expanded

Young writers need dedicated amounts of time and space (Fletcher & Portalupi, 2001) to tinker, try, and approximate their writing because "becoming a better writer requires that students [actually] write" (*Professional Knowledge*, 2016). Along with time and space to write, writers need access to high-quality writing instruction. This includes teachers composing and modeling their own writing, as well as the intentional selection of inspiring mentor texts (Calkins, 1994; Dorfman, Cappelli & Hoyt, 2017) that tend to genre, structure, voice, languaging, and the taking of syntactic risks. The time and space for self-expression is coupled with consistent and constructive feedback on writing in progress (Graves, 1994). However, this type of instruction must begin, as we witnessed in the brief portrait from Ms. Bautista's writing community, with a deep knowledge of who our students are, not just as writers but as human beings. What do we know about our students? What communities do they belong to? What matters most to them? Who are the important persons and places in their lives? Designing writing instruction, then, begins with a focus on who the writers are, what they have the potential to do, and the belief that we can teach our writers both strategies to improve their writing and tools to add to their existing linguistic and cultural repertoires.

Teachers Helping Students Become Better Writers

As teachers of young writers, our job is to demystify what writing is and what writers do. We can work with our young writers to read texts like writers (Fletcher, 2013; Ray, 1999) to understand the moves that writers make to tell stories, to enter into debates, to persuade, or to entertain. We can introduce students to the published writing and words of diverse writers, poets, and storytellers to show them examples of the many ways that authors compose. Through this exploration of writers and writing, we can discuss with students how writing happens beyond the walls of the classroom and can spill into their lives in powerful and purposeful ways.

Our work is to support young writers to understand that writing is a process not only for them, but also for the published authors whose work they are reading, and to see that they too are lifelong writers who can improve their craft within a supportive community of writers. Teachers in such supportive communities situate writing within their students' worlds because they "help our students see themselves as writers with stories to tell and ideas to share" (Newman, 2012, p. 25). They use mentor texts in bi/multilingual classrooms to demystify the writer's craft. Some premises guiding their writing instruction include:

- Young writers come to our classrooms with rich histories and with important stories and perspectives to share. They are storytellers, artists, dancers, musicians and creators of text—oral, written, and embodied.

- Young writers learn to use writing as a tool to explain, explore, examine, argue, amplify, and so much more.

- Young writers notice that writing lives and thrives beyond the classroom and is a tool for change—to raise consciousness of the lived conditions of their communities and the world.

- Young writers inquire about perspectives and languages different than their own and move "toward greater flexibility, so that they can write not just for their own intimates but for wider audiences." (*Professional Knowledge*, 2016)

In helping students to inquire, name, describe, and raise consciousness of their communities and the wider world, teachers may ask themselves: How do we prepare our writers to recognize the power in their writing? How do we illuminate the ways in which writing can be and is a tool for changing unjust conditions? How do we cultivate the storied lives and traditions of all our students?

Our work as teachers of young writers begins from the perspective and deeply held belief that our students come to our classrooms as writers with important stories to tell. Our young writers are raised and nurtured within communities where stories and storytelling are important intergenerational literacy practices passed on by elders and family members. These values and beliefs are challenged by restrictive curricula, policies, mandates, and political agendas that seek to reproduce the status quo by silencing and marginalizing the voices of our youth and their teachers.

In Ms. Bautista's classroom, and in the portraits of teachers you will meet across the chapters of this book, you will witness the power of writing communities in which young writers are provided with time and space to practice writing, are framed as writers, and are encouraged to write[bravely alongside teachers who teach fearlessly.]

How We Come to This Project

Throughout this book, we invite you, the reader, into a process of self-reflection and self-examination of your personal views and beliefs for cultivating young writers and nurturing their voices. If we are to make our writing classrooms spaces where our young writers can flourish, we must be open to this ongoing, inner process of interrogation in the service of our students. Alongside this invitation, we open up our lives to you, sharing personal stories from our childhoods and classroom experiences that foreground our responsibilities to our communities and our deep commitments to powerful literacy curricula for all learners.

Tracey T. Flores

As a second-generation Chicana growing up in Phoenix, Arizona, I was surrounded by the stories and *consejos* of my family. My immediate and my extended family shared stories when we would gather for meals, for holidays, or on any other occasion that brought us together. Their stories were always from their childhoods, and a majority of the memories they recounted involved moments spent with the family.

Of all the stories shared with me, the ones that have most vividly stayed with me came from my mother, Vivian. She told me many stories about her childhood and youth growing up in Holbrook, Arizona, surrounded by her family and with the dearest friends of her entire life. She recounted memories of attending daily mass with her mother, spending time with her nieces and nephews, and traveling with her high school band to Phoenix to march in parades. However, there is one story that my mother has shared time and time again, that as I've grown older, I have realized is part of my own story and history and shapes the way I come to my work as a teacher, teacher educator, and researcher.

When my mother was in elementary school, she had a teacher who punished her for speaking Spanish on the playground and in the classroom with her friends. The teacher would make her stay after school and write one-hundred times on the blackboard, "I will not speak Spanish on the playground." This was not a one-time punishment given by the teacher, but rather a regular occurrence, as my mother continued to speak Spanish, the language she had grown up speaking with her family, in class and on the playground. Each time my mother tells this story, I bear witness to the pain and shame she endured as a young girl that still stays with her to this day. As a result, my mother made the decision to not teach me and my sisters Spanish to protect us from this shame and ridicule.

While I was in the Multilingual/Multicultural (MLMC) teacher education program at Arizona State University, Arizona passed Proposition 203, which limited access to bilingual education for students learning English. Entering my own classroom as a fourth-grade English as a second language (ESL) teacher, I worked to ensure that my students never endured this same pain as multilingual children. However, I witnessed the social and academic harm of English-only policies and mandates (Garcia, Lawton & DeFigueiredo, 2012) in my classroom, as I would overhear students policing each other's language by calling attention to one another for speaking Spanish or other languages in the classroom.

Arizona's English-only mandates required that my students—multilingual children learning English as a second or third language—be placed in an English language development (ELD) classroom. In the ELD classroom, my students were mandated to receive four hours of discrete skill instruction in reading, writing, listening, and speaking. This limited their access to the same curricular opportunities as their native English-speaking peers, namely in the content areas (e.g., science) (Lillie, Markos, Arias & Wiley, 2012). The language and literacy instruction they did receive was often times based on an autonomous view of literacy (Street, 1995) in which instruction was decontextualized from their lived experiences and the linguistic practices of their homes and communities. At the core, these mandates positioned my students and families, a majority identifying as mixed-status, Spanish speakers and as Latinx, as deficient or in need of (re)mediation (Gutiérrez, Morales & Martinez, 2009).

During this time, I became a teacher consultant with the Central Arizona Writing Project (CAWP), where I formed a community with passionate writing teachers from across the state, working to create equitable writing classrooms. Within my ELD learning community, I invited my students and their families, the majority Latinx, to participate in an after-school family writing workshop in which we gathered to draw, write, and orally share our personal stories and histories (Flores, 2019). My students and their parents composed stories honoring friends, serving as tributes to beloved *abuelitos*, celebrating religious and cultural traditions, and naming their dreams for the future. Through the telling and composing of our personal stories and histories, we cultivated authentic relationships rooted in *confianza* (Alvarez, 2017).

From these workshops, I designed and facilitated Somos Escritoras/We Are Writers, a writing an art workshop that invites Latina girls in grades six to eight to share and perform stories from their lived experiences using art, theater, and writing as tools for self-reflection and self-examination. Our goal is to support girls to continue developing their writing while learning new tools to speak their truths, define themselves, and amplify their voices within a supportive community of Latina girls and women (Flores, 2023; 2021).

My commitment to this work and to this project is highly personal and political. My mother's language history, my experiences teaching alongside my students in restrictive language and literacy classrooms, and writing and sharing with Latinx families and girls in Somos Escritoras is what brings me to this current project. Their stories, voices, and experiences are woven into my teaching and research and are part of my own journey and story. I strive to prepare teachers to understand their role as advocates with and for their students, while creating classroom communities that center the languages, cultures, and identities of their students.

María E. Fránquiz

Like Virginia, I share with you, the reader, my wonderful *familia*. My *Mami* grew up in a poor *barrio* in Bayamón, Puerto Rico. She was the youngest of seven children and the only one to graduate from high school. My *Papi* grew up in the same *barrio*, was the oldest of thirteen children, and apprenticed to work in carpentry with his *Papi* after eighth grade. I was born and grew up in Puerto Nuevo, currently a densely populated *municipio* in the metropolitan area of San Juan. I recall our neighborhood as a working-class community in which telling stories was the way to socialize the younger generations about the values, histories, traditions, recipes, and remedies that were often excluded from the formal structures of schools, churches, and governments. Sharing memories of the past under Spanish colonization, descriptions of present American colonization, and dreams of the island's independence from colonialism were common stories heard in day-to-day conversational exchanges among parents, neighbors, aunts and uncles, older cousins, and visitors from other parts of the island. *Bochinche* (a term that means *chisme* for Mexican-American speakers or gossip for English speakers) was ubiquitous and often centered on community norms or provided a sense of personal and collective pride. I remember being absorbed in the *bochinche* and feeling such pride when the buzz involved people I knew—my grandfather sharing news of his harvest with neighbors, my *Papi* being promoted to sergeant in the US Army, my sister being cured of thrush with herbal medicines, or my *madrina* (godmother) touted as the best seamstress in our *municipio*. These stories were communicated in Spanish and represent a community discourse that worked itself into my reader and writer identities. As stated by Sonja Z. Pérez (2002) ". . . one of the reasons that people in the United States tell stories is to write themselves into the discourse of nationhood, to revise the official stories of the nation, the constitution of We the People" (p. 277). This type of authoring became particularly poignant for me as my childhood became a diasporic experience in the middle of my third grade.

From kindergarten to third grade, my teachers at Academia Santa Monica spoke Spanish, with the exception of one subject, English, taught by an Irish-Catholic nun. In March of my third grade, my *Papi* was transferred to Ft. Bragg, North Carolina. Initially, life in the eastern seaboard at St. Patrick's School was a humbling experience. My sister cried during morning prayers because she did not understand English and was subsequently retained in kindergarten. My *Papi* spent all of his free time that spring and summer teaching his children English.

It was hard for my *familia* to live on the mainland, and there were many more humbling moments, as my *Papi* was transferred to different army bases. One bitter memory I carried for years was inflicted by a Mexican-American teacher in El Paso, Texas. She made fun of my Puerto Rican Spanish language variant on the first day of school. When I asked her, "*¿Dónde puedo encontrar la parada de guaguas?* (Where can I find the bus stop?)," she answered, "Speak English. And the correct word for bus is *camión*." I assumed incorrectly that I could use Spanish in school. I also assumed that "*guaguas*" (buses) referred to the same vehicle in Puerto Rico and in El Paso, where there were many Spanish speakers. I was wrong on both counts.

My *familia* lived in many other linguistic and cultural contexts in California, Germany, and Alaska. Each relocation influenced our language and cultural ways. Since I went to college in the West, I became acquainted with the cultural nationalism of the Chicanx movement. Imagine, I was a Puerto Rican taking up Chicanx causes. Consequently, my friends called me a ChicaRican—not because I had mixed parentage, but because I had mixed cultural and political affiliations. While I was enrolled in classes in the Graduate School of Education at the University of California, Santa Barbara, I was selected to be one of two teaching assistants for the late César Chávez when he taught the Farm Labor History of California. This remarkable educational experience sealed my cultural and political hybrid identity as a ChicaRican and added richness to my diaspora consciousness. At the end of my graduate studies, I became a teacher consultant of the South Coast Writing Project (SCWriP). Years later, I worked with the leadership team of the National Writing Project and the English Department at the University of Puerto Rico in Mayagüez to revive the MayaWest Writing Project on the island. Presently, as a teacher educator and researcher, I bring to students the stories of my *familia* and my lived experiences as the seeds for writing their own stories.

Professional Knowledge for the Teaching of Writing: Theories of Teachers

The revised and expanded NCTE policy statement on *Professional Knowledge for the Teaching of Writing* (2016), written "by members for members," provides educators and teacher educators with an updated vision for the teaching of writing in K–12 classrooms. This revised statement, like the one from which it was first established, is rooted in the latest research and provides insights into what effective writing instruction might look like across a lifespan. The updated statement reflects the shifting modes and modalities for which individuals write and use writing in the different spaces of their everyday lives.

The revised statement serves as a resource for teachers and teacher educators as they work to become the type of teachers of writers that our students, families, and communities deserve. It provides a link between theory and practice for teachers and teacher educators to recognize the ways that theory can materialize into practice in increasingly diverse classrooms, and the ways that practice can and should inform theory. This statement is mindful of the ever-changing landscape of writing and learning to write, in and out of school, while continuing to highlight the value and importance of highly skilled teachers for our young writers in the classroom.

This is a guide, however, as the role of the teacher is central. Teachers are the ones who truly know their students, families, and communities, and work within different locations with specific contextualizing factors. Teachers are the ones who navigate each day, making decisions informed by the unique students who come to their classroom each and every day.

Professional Knowledge for the Teaching of Writing (2016) is not a script for teaching young writers. It is not a one-size-fits-all approach to teaching young writers. The statement offers principles that support teachers in the professional choices they make every single day. The statement stands on the shoulders of teachers who have had the courage and creativity to close their classroom doors and do the work of teaching and loving every child that becomes a part of their learning community. It is a testament to their advocacy, their fight, and their will to ensure that every child sees themselves as a reader, writer, and creator for change.

The Teachers of Young Writers

The heart of this book centers the stories, practices, and voices of elementary classroom teachers working in K–5 settings. These particular educators teach in schools located in Arizona and Texas. Each state has a unique context for the educational policies and programming offered to students and families, with different sociopolitical contexts and theoretical and practical approaches to teaching young writers. The history of this educational programming is also part of the larger story of the ways in which teachers across the United States are innovating practices within local and national language and literacy policies and mandates.

Language Context of Arizona

The official language of Arizona is English. The complexity of Arizona's language policies is contradictory. In the mid-1990s Ron Unz, a multimillionaire from the Silicon Valley, financed the California Proposition 227, "English for the Children" campaign, and characterized bilingual education as a failed and expensive experiment where children languished for years. His success in California inspired him to promote the passage of Proposition 203 in Arizona in 2000. English was declared as the official language of Arizona in 2006, and every school district was required to provide a four-hour model of structured English immersion (SEI) for students who were classified as "English Learners." Waivers from this rigid pedagogical approach were difficult for parents to obtain. Next, SB 1014 was passed in 2019. This law reduces the required hours of segregated English immersion from four to two hours for students in K–5. The new law is interpreted as allowing for alternative English instruction models such as dual-language or transitional bilingual education.

Bilingual Education Programs

A common premise for all bilingual education programs, including dual-language programs, is for instruction and assessment to be provided in two languages, for example, Spanish and English or Vietnamese and English. In early-exit or late-exit bilingual programs, two languages are used to transition to the dominant English program and transitioning is planned for the early or the upper elementary grades. Typically, early- and late-exit programs are comprised of students from immigrant or mixed-status families. While dual-language bilingual programs include this same population of students transitioning from home language to English, they also include monolingual English speakers transitioning to their second language.

Language Context of Texas

Texas does not have an official language policy. While 65 percent of Texans speak only English at home, a large number of Texas households speak Spanish. There are also significant numbers of Vietnamese and Chinese speakers. Along with Illinois, New Jersey, and New York, Texas is one of the only four states currently requiring bilingual education services for children who do not speak English at home. Bilingual education allows school districts to use the home language of students for reading and writing and for facilitating the development of bilingualism, biculturalism, and biliteracy. The Latinx population of Texas is young, with Latinx students accounting for more than half of the number of Texas students in the public-school system. At least, four bilingual education program models are offered at the elementary level to linguistically diverse students in Texas. These are English as a Second Language, Transitional Bilingual, English Immersion, and Two-Way Immersion or Dual-Language Education.

These are the contexts for the states where the six teachers highlighted in this book work with young writers from culturally and linguistically diverse backgrounds: in classroom settings, which are either English-only where instruction is delivered in English, or bilingual/dual-language classrooms in which students receive instruction in both English and Spanish. These teachers have varied years of experience with elementary students in these distinct settings, in different schools with differing sociopolitical contexts.

As educators, teacher educators, and scholars of literacy, we understand the high stakes that these language policies and resulting accountability measures place on teachers. Too often, this focus can cause a narrowing of the curriculum in favor of a rigid, skills-based approach to instruction in writing (Wohlwend, 2009). And, for some teachers, writing takes a back seat to "tested" subjects, being reduced to no more than short-answer responses to texts.

This book provides teachers and teacher educators with concrete examples of the ways that the six profiled educators (and others) are moving in a different direction: designing and implementing writing instruction that begins with the cultural, linguistic, and familial resources of young writers; centering their interests and voices; and extending writing beyond the classroom walls. The unique voices and perspectives of the teachers provide a contextualized approach to teaching young writers that can be used across grade levels, geographic regions, and district and state curriculum mandates. They each offer innovative ideas for working from within the walls of the classroom that all teachers of young writers in any context can bring into their own practice to develop powerful writing communities.

The Teachers:

Carmela Valdez, First-Grade Dual Language, Austin, Texas

Ms. Valdez is currently an early childhood, Dual-Language teacher and in her sixteenth year of teaching. She earned a Bachelor of Arts in theatre from the University of Texas at Austin and a Master of Education in early childhood education from Texas State University. Ms. Valdez is a teacher consultant (TC) of the Heart of Texas Writing Project (HTWP), and an affiliate of the National Writing Project (NWP), located in the College of Education at UT Austin. Since 2019, she has co-directed the Invitational Summer Institute for K–12 teachers and conducts bilingual writing workshops for Texas school districts. In 2021, Ms. Valdez received the Donald H. Graves Award for Excellence in the Teaching of Writing from the National Council of Teachers of English (NCTE). In 2022, she was awarded Teacher of the Year by the Austin Area Bilingual Association. She was also elected as a teacher representative to the NCTE Nominating Committee. Ms. Valdez is a passionate advocate for the rights of every multilingual student and believes language is a civil right.

Miriam Ortiz, Second-Grade, Bilingual Teacher, Manor, Texas

Originally from the U.S./Mexico border at Eagle Pass in Texas, Mrs. Ortiz has eleven years of teaching experience in Manor and Austin Independent School Districts (ISDs). She is a first-generation college graduate, and brings this experience to her classroom to create college-going pathways for her students, families, and their communities to thrive. Mrs. Ortiz currently serves Austin ISD's community of learners within the Multilingual Education Department as a multilingual specialist for elementary schools. In this role, she develops dual-language (DL) curriculum that reflects the biliteracy framework under a 90/10 DL program. She also provides professional learning for DL elementary teachers, modeling student-centered best practices and oracy strategies that lead children to biliteracy. She was awarded the honor of Teacher of the Year in 2014 and 2019 by her school district. Mrs. Ortiz has also been recognized as the NCTE 2021 Early Childhood Education Assembly's Early Literacy Master Teacher. For her, "children deserve a world of opportunities for infinite possibilities," and for living up to this perspective, she continues to honor the profession.

Sandra Springer, Third-Grade Bilingual Teacher, Austin, Texas

Mrs. Springer is a native of El Salvador. Being a survivor of a twelve-year civil war in her country contributed to her developing a critical consciousness toward social justice issues. Mrs. Springer completed a master's reading teaching certificate and a master's degree in bilingual and bicultural education at the University of Texas at Austin. For the last twenty-one years, she has worked in various models of bilingual education. She was honored twice by her colleagues as "Teacher of the Year," and was also named Austin Bilingual Teacher of the Year by the Austin Area Association for Bilingual Education. In 2017, she was honored as Texas Bilingual Teacher of the Year by the Texas Association for Bilingual Education, and in 2019, she was runner-up for the National Bilingual Teacher of the Year sponsored by the National Association for Bilingual Education. Mrs. Springer is a member of the NCTE Professional Dyads and Culturally Relevant Teaching (PDCRT) program and serves as the vice president of the Austin Area Association for Bilingual Educators (AAABE), where she has implemented "Pláticas," a co-learning space for teachers. She based the co-learning space on cross-generational teacher pláticas in which she participated with preservice, newly inducted, and veteran teachers for several years (see Fránquiz & Salinas, 2022).

Kerry Alexander, Fourth-Grade Teacher, Austin, Texas

For ten years, Mrs. Alexander has taught fourth-grade language arts and reading in Central Texas. As a classroom literacy educator, she focuses on putting learners' identities at the center of her practice and curriculum design. Most recently, Mrs. Alexander is working toward her doctorate in language and literacy studies at the University of Texas at Austin. Through critical, multimodal, and inquiry-based pedagogies, she embodies what she calls an act of *language artistry*: the relational, multimodal, meaning-making involved in designing for a more inclusive world. As a graduate student, Mrs. Alexander has developed a self-produced podcast series, *Coaching with Kerry*, focusing on community-teacher voices and stories. Additionally, she has a two-year appointment as equity chair at a local elementary school. Together, caregivers, teachers, and administrators ask: What is the community's vision for equity in literacy classrooms? Mrs. Alexander is a teacher consultant (TC) for the Heart of Texas Writing Project (HTWP) where she leads Saturday writing workshops for HTWP, and has led professional development sessions for teachers throughout the state.

Soledad Bautista, Fourth-Grade Dual-Language Teacher, Austin, Texas

Emigrating from Guadalajara, Mexico, to Texas as a young adult, Ms. Bautista has taught first, second, and fourth grade during her twelve years of teaching in the United States. To her classroom teaching, she brings experiences as a psychologist in Mexican hospitals and other institutions. She is a teacher consultant (TC) for the Heart of Texas Writing Project. Currently, Ms. Bautista is the director of professional development and outreach for Creative Waco, an organization that builds the relationship between businesses and creativity in that community. She is responsible for the launch of the first bilingual cohort in the nation for Air Collaborative. Her recent relocation to Waco, Texas, has reconnected her with her love of art, theater, and film. She strongly believes that if we have had to endure collective trauma due to the pandemic, there has to be a way to experience collective healing. A healing example is an HBO award-winning film, *When You Clean a Stranger's Home*. It was made for the 2021 Latinx Short Film Competition, and Ms. Bautista played a role in it. In this film, an individual story embraces and highlights the importance of every story. She believes that "multilingualism and multiculturalism are perhaps one of the strongest hopes we have to write a different history."

Christina Bustos, Fifth-Grade Teacher, Mesa, Arizona

Born and raised in Arizona, Ms. Bustos taught for nineteen years in grades three to eight in the cities of Phoenix, Tempe, and Mesa. Most recently, she added educational technology expertise to her responsibilities and serves as an ed-tech coach for Mesa Public Schools. She is also actively involved in the Mesa Education Association (MEA), the local affiliate of the Arizona Education Association (AEA), where she serves as the vice president and the committee chair for social and racial justice. She has been chosen to participate at the national level in the AEA initiatives for recruitment and retention of diverse educators. She represented MEA at the National Education Association 2022 Leadership Summit and participated in Leaders for Just Schools and NEA coconspirators for antiracist education. For NCTE, Ms. Bustos has created principles for teachers to create multimodal text sets that include books, audio/video read-alouds, podcasts, recorded interactions with authors, websites, articles, timelines, and song. In all her efforts, she is an advocate for learners to develop healthy and well-rounded understandings on a variety of topics.

As noted earlier, this book is written in response to and connection with the most recent revisions to the NCTE position paper on *Professional Knowledge for the Teaching of Writing*. We provide elementary school educators, future educators, teacher educators, and classroom researchers with concrete examples of effective writing pedagogy for all young writers, with particular emphasis on engaging culturally and linguistically diverse young writers and their repertories. Throughout the book, we highlight the voices and stories of these six classroom educators, teaching in varied settings—from bilingual, dual-language, and English-only contexts—and their work alongside their young writers. Through classroom portraits, each educator shares examples of their pedagogical approaches for cultivating young writers and the ways they organize, design, and facilitate writing curriculum to meet the unique needs of their students. These teachers share the ways they use mentor texts to facilitate writing and performing, examples of multimodal writing artifacts from students written in different genres (e.g., narrative, how-to pieces, poems, etc.), strategies to center students' personal interests in various writing opportunities, and approaches for engaging students' families and communities through publishing and public performances (i.e., young writers' celebrations).

Development of This Book

We ourselves have gone through a process of becoming critical teacher educators and scholars. For the purposes of this book, critical teacher educators are those who identify, acknowledge, and lift up the voices of extraordinary teachers of writing who are invested in elevating the voices of all their students. Critical teacher educators and scholars highlight the practices of teachers who examine what counts as power in writing and reimagine the multiple ways to expand provincial views with their students. As such, we present in this book portraits of these six extraordinary elementary school teachers. The portraits reveal how they create space for students to write, reframe, revise, publish, and celebrate their cultural and linguistic strengths and complexities. The methods of portraiture require the portraitists (i.e., the authors of this book) to examine the intersection between self and the teachers to consider the powers that may be inherent in their relationships (Chapman, 2006; Fránquiz, Salazar & DeNicolo, 2012; Lawrence-Lightfoot, 2005; Lawrence-Lightfoot & Davis, 1997). Portraits examine deeply the ebb and flow of feelings, discoveries, and commitments that students and teachers express during normalized, as well as challenging, times.

In Chapter Two, we provide portraits of Ms. Bustos's fifth-grade classroom in Arizona and Ms. Alexander's fourth-grade classroom in Texas. The teachers have sketched the environment in which they invite their students to write, revise, and publish their stories. They also share how they use the physical space and the material culture of the classroom, including mentor texts, to provide the time and models necessary for deep thinking and composing.

Mrs. Ortiz's bilingual second-grade classroom and Mrs. Springer's bilingual third-grade classroom are highlighted in Chapter Three. Underscored in this chapter are the ways in which each teacher organizes projects or units of study and the types of writing children generate. The two teachers plan writing lessons that may be completed in Spanish and/or English, and they integrate subject area learning so that students write for different purposes.

In Chapter Four, we highlight the classroom practices of first-grade teacher Ms. Valdez and fourth-grade teacher Ms. Bautista. Both teachers use a writer's workshop approach to teaching young writers in their respective classrooms in different geographical areas of a large urban metropolitan city in Central Texas. We focus on the ways each teacher plans for the assessment of students' writing through daily writing conferences that involve sitting alongside their students to document their strategies while providing in-the-moment teaching to support their development as writers.

At the end of each chapter, you will find a section titled, "Pause, Reflect & Write." In this section, we offer questions that invite you to pause *and* reflect on your own pedagogical practices and beliefs and classroom learning community, to envision how you might integrate new learnings from these teacher portraits into your current teaching context. We encourage you to write down your reflections, questions, and ideas, and to share them as part of a study group or with a critical friend who can support you and push you in envisioning new possibilities for your students and your classroom teaching.

The concluding chapter to this book links together the exemplary practices of these six teachers who specifically plan for students to use their linguistic and cultural repertoires to write their voices and identities and those of their families and communities into the elementary language arts curriculum. At the end of the book, we provide an annotated bibliography, with some of our favorite resources curated by the educators featured in this book. Along with our six teachers' recommendations, we provide our own suggestions from our K–12 writing classrooms, in after-school community writing spaces, and alongside preservice teachers in our methods courses to support your work in cultivating multilingual writers.

Pause, Reflect & Write:

- What are your earliest memories of learning to write? How did you learn? What was challenging? When did you feel successful? Why?
- Who was your audience? How was your writing shaped by your imagined reader?
- What approaches do you draw on to support the growth of young writers?
- What experiences do students need to see themselves as writers? How do I provide these experiences?

Chapter Two

Designing a Writing Community: Time, Space, and Material Culture

*A*ll writers need time *and* space (Fletcher & Portalupi, 2001) to develop their craft and find their writing process. Let's start by thinking about time. Like athletes, actors, musicians and artists, writers need focused time engaging in their craft, as practice is necessary to build their writing muscles and confidence as writers. This also suggests that writers need time learning alongside an expert—their teacher—who can model their own writing process, talk through parts where they too become "stuck," and explicitly teach writing to support students in becoming skillful and strategic writers. Our young writers need time to "do" the things that writers do—to research, explore, draft, talk about their writing, edit, revise, publish, and more. This requires that our writers have a consistent and extended amount of time each day devoted to writing.

In considering space, we often think about the physical space and the ways that we design our classroom environments for teaching and learning. This tends to include the placement of furniture and involves the ways we organize the nooks and crannies of our rooms to encourage the flow of ideas, collaboration, and dialogue. What we do with the space in our classroom can invite, or not invite, students into learning and writing. The ways that we organize the space in our learning communities for writers to engage in writing and the practices that writers do matters. Therefore, many researchers document the material culture of writing classrooms (Fránquiz & Salazar, 2004; Johnson, 1980).

The material culture of the classroom describes the objects, artifacts, architecture, and design of a learning community. Material culture refers to wall displays, posters, symbols, and images that can be found around the room and can be representative of the local or national traditions. Additionally, it is important to note that what is present in the space is just as important as what is absent. By close observation of a learning community, you can begin to gain an understanding of the values, beliefs, and ways that students and teachers gather in a teaching and learning community.

In this chapter, we share portraits of two learning communities located in the southwestern region of the United States: Arizona and Texas. Both classrooms are in schools situated in large K–12 school districts serving culturally and linguistically diverse students, families, and communities. Both classrooms are English-medium classrooms in which instruction occurs throughout the school day in English. In each classroom, we see the classroom space and the material culture of the classroom as vital parts of these writing communities. The teachers co-design the space *with* and *for* students to grow as writers and thinkers. In these classrooms, young writers engage in "writing that matters" (Ghiso, 2011), through which they can begin to author their lives in new ways.

Within these classrooms, Ms. Bustos's and Mrs. Alexander's teaching practices and the material culture of their classrooms are rooted in an understanding, as described in the NCTE position statement on *Professional Knowledge for the Teaching of Writing* (2016), these teachers understand that "writing and reading are related" reciprocal processes that are connected to one another. To make these explicit connections across their literacy instruction, Ms. Bustos and Mrs. Alexander consistently carve out time each day for writing instruction. They intentionally organize their classroom space to facilitate collective dialogue and community building through proximity, ritual, and routine. These teachers have curated and created a robust classroom library to provide their students with access to literature and multimodal texts written in a variety of formats. These books support students' growing understanding of genre and structure as they learn to compose for different purposes and audiences. Using books as a vehicle for dialogue, Ms. Bustos and Mrs. Alexander create many opportunities throughout the school day for students to examine the different themes that are relevant to their lives. They seek to support their young writers in composing texts to speak to the issues that are most important to them and to understand that their voices and writing matter in *and* beyond the walls of the classroom.

Ms. Bustos

I started to wonder who had the right to write the stories because it shouldn't be someone who didn't experience it. It should be someone who knows firsthand and comes from that community.

—Ms. Christina Bustos

Born and raised in Arizona, Ms. Bustos has spent nineteen years teaching in K–8 schools across the state. Ms. Bustos comes from a proud family with strong values and ties to the local community. As a first-generation college graduate, Ms. Bustos credits her parents for instilling in her the importance of learning through reading. An avid book reader, she loves sharing books with her students and friends, something that she learned from her father. In books, she has found a place to learn about her culture, community, and injustices impacting people from marginalized communities. Reading opened her mind to the inequities present in the world, and it is in books that she recognized an absence of literature and texts about Mexican Americans and people, like herself, who identified as mixed heritage.

Ms. Bustos took this awareness with her to college, where she enrolled in the Multilingual/Multicultural (MLMC) Elementary Education Teaching Program at Arizona State University. There she learned about theories like funds of knowledge (Moll, Amanti, Neff & González, 1992; Gonzalez, Moll & Amanti, 2005), which highlighted for her the rich contributions that exist in the homes and communities of students and in which she saw in herself. These theories provided her with words to speak about her passions and put them into practice alongside her future students. She always believed and knew of the gifts and resources of bilingual and multilingual students, and the theories she learned provided a framework for her teaching. It was in this program where she was introduced to the power of using literature as mentor texts to teach young writers to develop their craft, share their stories, and amplify their voices.

In her teaching, Ms. Bustos draws upon her upbringing, her love of literature, and her college experiences to develop a writing curriculum that is relevant to her diverse students' lives. She believes, that "the only group that can tell your story is your group, the only person that can tell your personal story is you and one important way to make meaning from the themes in your life is through literacy." Ms. Bustos provides students with time and space daily to explore culturally relevant literature that is connected to their lives to inspire personal writing. Together, through their daily reading and writing, they cultivate a community of writers empowered to share their stories.

Luis Moll: Funds of Knowledge

In 2019, Luis C. Moll explained during his acceptance of the Distinguished Scholar Lifetime Achievement Award from the Literacy Research Association, that "the emphasis of the funds of knowledge work has been to develop both theory and methods through which educators can approach and document the funds of knowledge of families and represent them on the basis of the knowledge, resources, and strengths they possess, thus challenging deficit orientations that are so dominant, in particular, in the education of working-class children." The idea is to represent family and community knowledge as important resources for teaching, writing, and learning in academic environments.

A Vibrant Community Full of Stories: Ms. Bustos's Learning Community

Walking into Christina Bustos' fifth-grade learning community in Mesa, Arizona, you are surrounded by material culture in a sea of colors. Papel picado, made from tissue paper, in bright pink, orange, teal, purple, and yellow is hung around the perimeter of the room. Black and white bookshelves, tall and short, are stacked with bins filled with various picture books, and chapter books line the walls. Picture books with their covers facing out like cereal boxes in the cereal aisle include *A Gift of Gracias: The Legend of Altagracia* (Alvarez, 2005), *Abuelita's Heart* (Cordova, 2008), *Dreamers* (Morales, 2018), *Out of Wonder: Poems Celebrating Poets* (Alexander, Colderley & Wenworth, 2017), *Turning Pages: My Life Story* (Sotomayor, 2018), *Our House Is on Fire: Greta Thurnberg's Call to Save the Plant* (Winter, 2019), and titles spanning different genres. Chapter books include: *Crossover* (Alexander, 2019), *Tortilla Sun* (Cervantes, 2014), *Among the Hidden* (Haddix, 2000), *The Color of My Words* (Joseph, 2000), and *Harbor Me* (Woodson, 2018). On the walls, student work and anchor charts are posted, documenting and celebrating learning. Small lap pillows and lap desks sit on the floor. All these colors create an inviting and joyful feeling of warmth, happiness, and inspiration.

Student desks are intentionally placed in small groups to facilitate conversations and cooperative learning. Individual book bins hold teacher-recommended and student-selected texts. Along with these books, there are books displayed on the gutter of the whiteboard, books in bins below the whiteboard, and books stacked in piles on the teacher's desk.

FIGURE 2.1. Map of Ms. Bustos's Learning Community

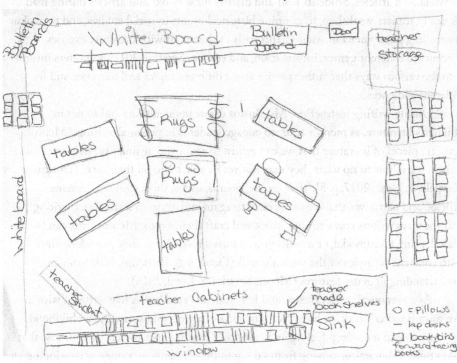

Nestled between all the color, books, and students' desks is the class meeting area. Large rugs are placed in the center, inviting students to take their places on the floor, alongside their peers. This space is just right for students to gather and lean in close for a read-aloud, teacher mini-lessons, discussions, and sharing writing. Writing materials are located close by. There are decorated clipboards, a few bins holding writer's notebooks, and extra stickies and pencils—all the tools writers need to compose.

The material culture of Ms. Bustos's learning community is alive, welcoming, and warm. This is a community filled with stories. This is a community that values stories. This is a community where young writers have the space, time, and tools they need to write. This is a community where young writers are encouraged to craft their stories alongside all the voices in the room.

"Start with Their Stories"

Ms. Bustos believes that to grow writers and support them in developing their writing process, we must "start with *their* stories." One way that Ms. Bustos and her writers start to reflect on their own stories is through daily reading and discussion of children's and young adult literature. This includes poetry and short story anthologies, op-eds, and Newsela.com articles. Students read and discuss these books and articles during read alouds in readers' workshop, to examine historical events in social studies, and to explore compelling phenomena in science. This daily engagement with literature exposes students to different genres, information, and stories (Serafini, 2011) and offers insight into the various ways that authors write about different topics and purposes and for different audiences.

During writing instruction, Ms. Bustos draws upon authors and topics in children's literature, as mentor texts, to engage students in personal writing. "Mentor texts are pieces of literature that we can return to again and again as we help our young writers learn how to do what they may not yet be able to do on their own" (Dorfman, Cappelli & Hoyt, 2017, p. 5). They are the poems, songs, short stories, magazine articles, and narratives that we come back to again and again to learn about writing and the ways writers come to their work and craft their words. Mentor texts can be digital, print, multimodal, or a collection of mixed modalities. They provide writers with concrete examples of the author's craft (Fletcher & Portalupi, 2001) and an understanding of genre features (Moses, Serafini & Loyd, 2016).

As a community, Ms. Bustos and her students "read books like writers," with an eye toward writer's craft, to learn from the gifts of a well-told story, and a childhood memory shared with deep feeling and emotion. "Reading like writers" is a process that takes time and practice, moving from taking in the elements of a story to developing an eye toward a writer's craft. Through repeated immersion into diverse texts and practice, the young writers in Ms. Bustos's class "try on" craft moves within the personal and informational stories they are composing with purpose and audience in mind.

In the next sections, we take a seat in Ms. Bustos's learning community as her writers join in a read-aloud of *When I Was Young in the Mountains* (Rylant, 1982). We learn how Ms. Bustos has intentionally selected this story as a mentor text to teach the writer's craft of using repeating lines and lyrical verses to capture personal memories. Finally, we see her writers as they engage in their own writing of personal memories inspired by the text, the teacher model, and their conversations.

Drawing on Mentor Texts to Inspire Personal Writing

This learning community's meeting area is a cozy and inviting space for students to listen to the story that their teacher, Ms. Bustos, reads at the front of the room. Students sit on the carpet in the meeting area, some in chairs, others on the floor. Seated on a chair facing students, Ms. Bustos shares the classic story *When I Was Young in the Mountains,* written by Cynthia Rylant (1982). The book was selected for the Caldecott Honor, and the story recounts the author's fond childhood memories growing up in the Appalachian Mountains. These memories include foods prepared by her grandmother, going to the local store to buy a mound of butter, and summer nights spent on the front porch with her grandparents. Throughout the lyrically written story, the author uses repeated lines, such as "When I was young in the mountains," to weave together the emotions and love embedded within her memories.

Ms. Bustos selected this book as a mentor text to teach her fifth-grade writers how to write with emotion, by evoking familial memories from their childhood that remind them of the joy present in their everyday lives. Although this book is set in the Appalachian Mountains, in a very different time and context from the dry desert of Arizona, the memories shared by the author are relatable and center special cultural and familial traditions and memories through the eyes of a young person. For Ms. Bustos, this story serves the purpose of engaging her young writers in personal writing while trying the writer's craft of using repeating lines and lyrical verses to capture memories.

Before she begins, she reveals to her students that this is one of her favorite stories to share and that it is one that was shared with her when she was in college. She opens the book and reads the first page,

> When I was young in the mountains,
> Grandfather came home in the evening covered with the black dust of a coal mine.
> Only his lips were clean, and he used them to kiss the top of my head" (n.p.).

The illustration shows the author meeting her grandfather at the door, where he is dressed in his dirty work clothes. She is looking up at him while he leans over to kiss the top of her head. Ms. Bustos shows her class this illustration. Then, she pauses and looks at her students and tells them a story about her own father that connects to this memory. She says, "My dad worked in the city, he did a lot of things, but one of his jobs was in streets and sanitation—he was a garbage man. I remember him coming home after work, entering through our garage, and heading straight to the shower. I never saw him right when he got home, only after he showered." She smiles, looking up as if remembering those moments. She finishes, "This reminds me of my dad and his work."

As Ms. Bustos continues, she stops on various pages, telling stories, sharing memories, and making connections from her own life to the story. On a page about a memory of a family dinner of "hot corn bread, pinto beans, and fried okra," she weaves in her own memories about dinners shared with her own family. Ms. Bustos explains how the foods in this story may be traditional staples that are part of the author's memories growing up in the Appalachian region of the United States. She tells students that this reminds her of the traditional foods prepared by her mother and grandmother for their family dinners. For her, as a bicultural Chicana, they ate tortillas, refried beans, and goulash. She describes these as important food staples in her family that fed everyone.

Each time Ms. Bustos shares a memory, she adds a bit more detail and lifts lines and words from the book to orally model for her students how she might write from her memories in the way that the author wrote from hers. While reading the author's words describing her memories of listening to the sounds of frogs singing at dusk and waking in the morning to the cowbells outside her window, Ms. Bustos intentionally stops to point out to students how she would draw on this craft move in writing about her own memories. She says, "If I were to write this, I would start with the author's words, 'When I was young in the Mountains' that she repeats throughout the story. I would change mountains to Tempe because that is where I grew up. Think about how you would share your memory using the author's repeated line to share your memories." She orally models what this would sound like. She says, "When I was young in Tempe, we listened to cicadas and crickets sing at dusk, and woke to a lawn mower outside our window in the morning." She turns the page and continues reading.

Finally, Ms. Bustos reaches the last page of the book, reading each word slowly, pausing to let each word sit in the air. "When I was young in the mountains, I never wanted to go to the oceans, and I never wanted to go to the desert. I never wanted to go anywhere else in the world, for I was in the mountains. And that was always enough." She closes the book and asks students to turn to their partners and share their thinking and noticings about the memories the author shared and the structure of the book.

After students share for a few minutes with their partners, she signals for them to end their conversations. Once she notices that students have finished speaking, she says, "Now, using this text as a model, we are going to begin gathering childhood memories from our own lives to create a story similar to this book. I want you to think about the memories that you would choose from your life. Think about the people, foods, and moments that are always with you. These are ideas to jot down for your story." She scans their faces as she is giving directions. Some students are looking at her and nodding, and others are already beginning to jot ideas in their notebooks as she continues, "Before we go back to our tables, let's share some of our ideas with our partners." Students turn and begin sharing with one another.

As the students share, they engage in dialogue around their memories and ideas. As they orally share and jot down ideas, this dialogue supports them in extending their thinking and adding more details. It serves as a form of rehearsal for the longer writing they will do once they gather all their memories and ideas. This practice of engaging with other writers is important for developing ideas and learning from others. It lifts the level of writing in the room and lays a foundation for students to recognize that writing is not a solitary act (Gee, 1996), but one that takes place through interactions and alongside other writers (Calkins, 1994). In other words, writing is relational, creating relationships between ideas and with others in the learning community (Murray, 2015).

Finally, Ms. Bustos signals for her students' attention and gives them instruction to move into independent writing time. She says, "Now that you have had a chance to talk to your friends, we will go back to our desks to begin to draft our stories. Cynthia Rylant's text will be a model for how you can organize your memories and ideas. But, your story will be specific for you."

After talking with her peers, one student, Grace, wrote about her childhood memories with her family and friends in New Mexico. Grace was not born in New Mexico. She moved there as a small child. It wasn't until she moved to Arizona, where her parents were originally from, that she gained a new appreciation for New Mexico. After Ms. Bustos's read-aloud, Grace decided to write her piece, titled, "When I Was Young in New Mexico," where she describes all the things that she loves about the state. This includes the many hot air balloons and the winter snow that turned the soccer park a fluffy white.

FIGURE 2.2. "When I Was Young in New Mexico" Draft

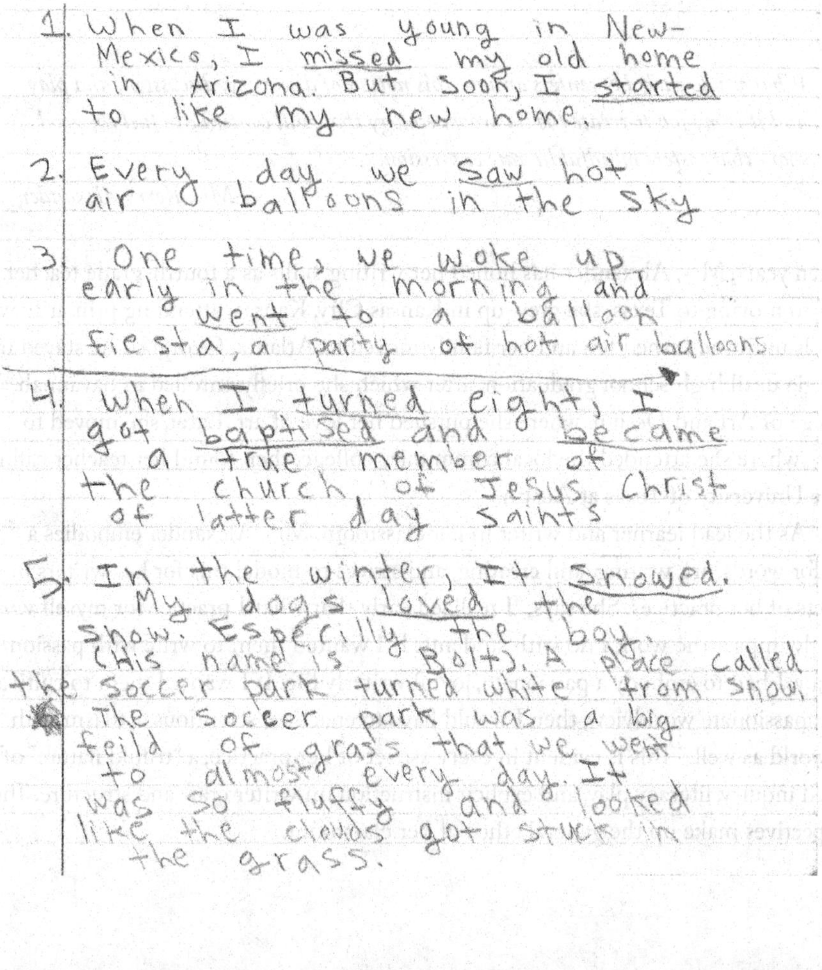

1. When I was young in New Mexico, I missed my old home in Arizona. But soon, I started to like my new home.

2. Every day we saw hot air balloons in the sky

3. One time, we woke up early in the morning and went to a balloon fiesta, a party of hot air balloons

4. When I turned eight, I got baptised and became a true member of the church of Jesus Christ of latter day saints

5. In the winter, It snowed. My dogs loved the snow. Especilly the boy. (His name is Bolt). A place called the soccer park turned white from snow. The soccer park was a big feild of grass that we went to almost every day. It was so fluffy and looked like the clouds got stuck in the grass.

Ms. Bustos's selection of literature connected to her students' childhood memories and provided a platform for them to reflect on their experiences and draft personal writing that was meaningful and relevant to their lives. During her read-aloud, Ms. Bustos purposefully stopped throughout to model for students the ways in which she connected to the texts by orally sharing memories from her childhood. As she read, she included more details, drawing from the repeated line, "When I was young," to frame the ways in which she spoke about her memories. Her model served as an example for how they might try this in their own writing. After she finished reading the story, Ms. Bustos provided students with time and space, or timespace (Compton-Lilly & Halverson, 2014), to engage in dialogue with their peers. This practice allowed them to rehearse ideas before getting them down on paper. In Ms. Bustos's teaching, we see the emphasis on stories, storytelling, and dialogue, and how each of these practices provides a scaffold and tool for her young writers to draw upon in writing from their emotions and experiences.

Mrs. Alexander

> *What we do each day centers around this notion of discovery, discussion, and play, and it is my job to create the classroom ecology that will continue to fuel the good work that fosters mindful literate expression.*
>
> *—Mrs. Kerry Alexander*

For ten years, Mrs. Alexander has honed her writing skills as a fourth-grade teacher. Prior to moving to Texas, she grew up in Kansas City, Kansas, attending primarily white schools until she turned ten and her family moved to Atlanta, Georgia. She stayed in Georgia until high school graduation, after which she briefly enrolled in Savannah College of Art and Design, where she pursued her love of art. Later, she moved to Texas, where she attended the local community college, then found her teacher calling at the University of Texas at Austin.

As the lead learner and writer in her classroom, Mrs. Alexander embodies a love for words, art, writing, and creating, and strives to model this for her writers in all aspects of her practices. She says, "I realized early that what I practice for myself would directly impact the work I do with students. If I wanted them to write with passion and joy, I had to embody a passionate, joyful writerly life. If I wanted them to cultivate a compassionate worldview, then I would have to enact conscientious activism with the world as well." This is evident in every aspect of her practice, a "trifold nature" of shared inquiry, literacy play, and explicit instruction on writer craft and structure. These perspectives make up the general ethos of her classroom.

Her love of words and writing brought her to the Heart of Texas Writing Project (HTWP) in 2010. The HTWP is a local affiliate of the National Writing Project (NWP). It was during this life-changing summer that her belief in writing as "not isolated, not rote, not simply for Standard American English skills, but for life" was nurtured and transformed. As a teacher consultant, Mrs. Alexander has worked with the local district to write and present workshops for K–8 teachers on writing workshops. She continues to work with the HTWP to promote the tenets put forth by the NWP and the National Council of Teachers of English (NCTE).

Mrs. Alexander's Classroom: Engaging in the Practices of Writers

Alive and full of energy and creativity, Mrs. Alexander's learning community is a welcoming space for students to learn and grow together. She organizes her room to encourage collaborative learning, thinking, and problem solving across the day. Her classroom is packed with an inviting material culture for her students: watercolor paints, typewriters, Chromebooks, paper of all colors and sizes, string, magnetic poetry, and literature (commercially published and student created) lining the walls and shelves. Titles of Young Adult (YA) literature books on the shelves include: *Mockingjay* (Collins, 2014), *The Maze Runner* (Dashner, 2010), *Merci Suárez Changes Gears* (Medina, 2018), *Ghost* (Reynolds, 2017), and *The Dreamer* (Ryan, 2012). Stacked next to these books are picturebooks, which include: *Yesterday I Had the Blues* (Frame, 2008), *The Upside Down Boy* (Herrera, 2006), *Love as Strong as Ginger* (Look, 1999), and *Grandfather's Journey* (Say, 2008).

Every inch of the classroom is useful to students and an important part of learning. Students keep their personal belongings in their backpacks and use individual mailboxes to hold their notebooks and writing portfolios. To make space and time to accommodate small-group learning as well as one-on-one conferring, the furniture in the fourth-grade space is very sparse. The primary meeting area for the learning community, which they have named the "living room," is centrally located in the middle of the classroom. It is surrounded by student desks in a U-shape to ensure face-to-face interactions no matter the activity or where students are seated. This design allows for Mrs. Alexander to move about the room with her traveling whiteboard and notebook to join conversations, provide support as needed, and assess progress.

Mrs. Alexander's room is a living history of the thinking, learning, and writing that she and her students do together throughout the long timespace of the school year. Rituals and routines are an important part of the ways in which Mrs. Alexander and her students live and learn as a community. Students look forward to dedicated and extended time for reading and writing, to grow in their craft. This is a space, rich with enthusiasm for the arts, inquiry, and writing that grows with endless possibilities as each day, week, and month of the year unfolds.

FIGURE 2.3. Map of Ms. Alexander's Learning Community

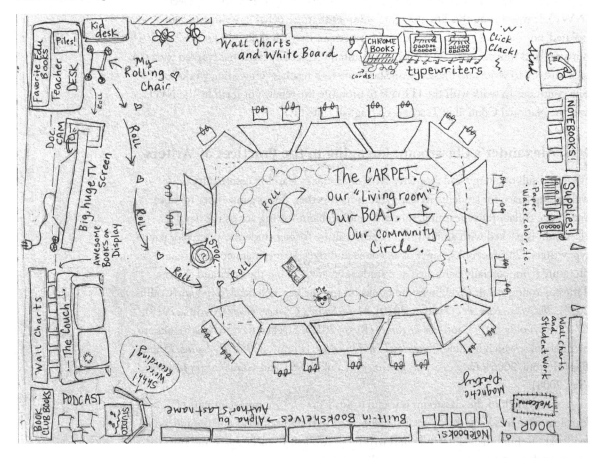

In the next sections, we examine closely the ways Mrs. Alexander and her students co-constructed life in their classroom during language arts. Descriptions trace how literacy practices of listening, speaking, reading, writing, and visually representing were experienced each day beginning with morning meetings in this fourth-grade class. From a dynamic flow of rich literacy practices established across the year, self-selected topics on social issues emerged and were augmented with texts, photos, discussions, and actions.

Morning Meeting: A Place for Writers to Begin Their Day

At the heart of Mrs. Alexander's teaching practice is the daily community morning meeting. Her morning meetings are not based upon a scripted program. Rather, they are born out of the need to connect and collaborate, to come together as a community that listens, learns, and examines life and the world together. In *Life in a Crowded Place:*

Making a Learning Community (Peterson, 1992), the author discusses the importance of ritual, routine, and ceremony in classrooms. He writes:

> But ceremony becomes very important when students are expected to construct meaning on their own and with others. Assuming responsibility for their own learning and not merely acting out someone else's plan calls upon students to focus their attention. Where study is concerned, ceremony brings about an internal readiness, pushing aside that which might interfere and helping students to participate wholeheartedly by concentrating thought and feeling on the work at hand. (p. 16)

The morning meeting in Mrs. Alexander's fourth-grade learning community is one of the ceremonies that she has co-constructed with her students. Her main goals are to foster togetherness in community, immersion into a relevant literacy, discussion and reflection, and time and space to synthesize individually and creatively. Together, members of the community negotiate their timespace, through the literature and texts that are read, shared, and discussed. This includes extended dialogue and personal writing.

In Table 2.1, Mrs. Alexander describes the critical components of the daily morning meetings that she facilitates in her learning community. These meetings are a space for students to gather in community as they start their day. It is a time to listen and be heard. She sets aside extended amounts of time and space for the community to practice how they receive each other's words, sometimes using a speaking stone. The community ritual includes the ways they sit and listen to each other, and the teacher modeling how to listen and receive through intentional oral language and body language. Students co-construct the different routines that are part of their meetings, negotiating and coming to consensus to meet the needs and concerns of every member of the community. As they grow together throughout the year, they revisit different aspects of their agreed-upon routines and rituals to ensure they are meeting their collective goals and revising if necessary.

Planting Seeds of Resistance

To capture a holistic portrait of the ways in which Mrs. Alexander orchestrates the daily morning meeting and contextualizes writing in her fourth-grade learning community, we provide an example of Mrs. Alexander and her students as they come together for morning meeting. We start with her students entering the classroom and moving to the classroom "living room" to begin their day together. This meeting, took place midway through the school year, and we can observe the routines that Mrs. Alexander and her students have co-constructed to ensure that the time is meaningful and productive.

TABLE 2.1. Mrs. Alexander describes the critical components of the daily morning

MY CRITICAL COMPONENTS	Thoughts...
Daily	Morning meetings are the **first thing** we attend as a class. It is an expected, daily part of our community.
Gathering Together	**Proximity and togetherness** is vital. We need to see each other, hear each other, and practice the nature of shared discussion. We always bring writer's notebooks.
Listening	**How we listen**—not just to respond, but to acknowledge another person's perspective, story, comment, or contribution—is a yearlong (and life-long) process. This is critical. When we listen to others, and when we learn to share opinion, difference, and disagreement wisely, we are on our way.
Sharing	**Circle:** This is a time to see all eyes and pass a speaking stone. It can be used in critical discussions, to reconnect or restore a centeredness, or to play group games. **Cluster:** This is a time to share a discussion more *authentically*—based on a video, a text, or a prompt—and practice how to sit where each of us is able to concentrate (including on chairs), have the freedom to manage our own bodies, and wait for our turn to participate.
Invitation	This is a preplanned, meaningful-for-the-group, DOING that connects to the students' lives, the business of the day, or an ongoing issue or practice. Examples might include a shared whole text, an excerpt, a language experience (e.g., a sentence or quote), an orally shared story, a play with words, a short video, a student spotlight, a game, an audio recording (e.g., podcast), current events, listings—anything that INVITES continued thought and fuels discussion.
Ten Minutes (Read, Write & Draw)	This is MY personal, critical component. Because learning to listen to our own thoughts, to write to think, to get centered before the directives begin, is a CRITICAL, humanizing practice, I include these ten minutes each day to close our meeting. I give this TIME to *read, write, or draw* back to the world in a personal and creative way because it is a necessity for a thinker.
Teacher Modeling	**Always, always, always:** • Using mindful, compassionate language. • Thinking out loud about issues and struggles from my own life and practice and community. • Listening for and leaning into student noticings, questions, and ideas for our togetherness. • Allowing humor and familiarity. • Writing or leaving little notes for students during R,W, D (read, write, draw).

As Mrs. Alexander's students enter their classroom in Portable Five, located across the school's playground, they chat about things that have happened since their previous day. Mixed with this conversation is laughter while they place their backpacks, jackets, and personal belongings on hooks in the back of the room. After each student puts their belongings away, they find their writer's notebooks, along with a pencil or pen, and make their way to the meeting area—the community "living room" carpet—for their daily morning meeting. This space is social, communal, and familial. Over the course of the year, the "living room" gives Mrs. Alexander a chance to connect with children and parents as they enter the room, monitor the general mood and affect, and *listen in*. The opportunity to read the room and truly listen to students is a critical aspect that sets the stage for their morning meeting and the work in which they will engage as a learning community.

In their classroom living room, some students lie down, chins on their hands, notebooks open in front of them. Other students lean on the legs of the desks that line their living room area, and others lean in with peers. As each student settles into their places on the living room carpet, Mrs. Alexander joins them.

Seated alongside students, Mrs. Alexander calls their attention by sounding a chime. Conversations die down, and students adjust their bodies to give her their attention. She brings different pieces of literature and texts to the meeting. This can take on many modes, many forms. Sometimes she brings a quote from what she is currently reading, some poetry, a news article from *News ELA*, or a piece of art. Mrs. Alexander selects literature and texts that she believes might spark their attention and curiosity, opening dialogue toward writing rooted in the worlds they are living and creating (Dyson, 1993; 2013).

On this morning, Mrs. Alexander projects the front page of a Newsela.com article titled "Cities around the world participate in women's marches and protests" on the large screen. This article was published on January 23, 2018, three days after the second women's march, a global protest advocating for women's rights and human rights. The first march, which took place in January 2017, occurred a day after President Donald Trump's inauguration. The women's march was organized in direct response and protest of Trump and his administration's attack on reproductive, civil, and human rights. This second march, occurring one year later, had been a topic of conversation in Mrs. Alexander's classroom.

Mrs. Alexander had prepared for the discussion and begins by passing out a hard copy of the article to each student. They engage in a shared reading of the article, discussing vocabulary, text structure, and content. After this initial reading and discussion, Mrs. Alexander invites students into a three-minute "quickwrite" reflection. The "quickwrite" allows students time to process and respond independently in writing (Rief, 2002; 2018) before sharing their thinking with a partner. Through quickwrites, students can rehearse what they might share with a partner. A teacher might also include a sentence frame to scaffold writing and language.

FIGURE 2.4. One of the Women's Marches held in cities across the world.

Photo: Credit: iStock.com/FG Trade.

Once students finish their quickwrites, Mrs. Alexander turns some solo piano music on Pandora and students begin their ten minutes of "Read, Write, and Draw." Students write as the room becomes quiet and the music plays in the background. During the "Read, Write, and Draw," students have choice of what they will write *and* how they will write. They follow their own personal writing projects on self-selected topics. Some students design graphic novels. Others write shape poetry of cats or trees. One student writes her opinion of Trump. Mrs. Alexander does not dictate the writing that students follow during this time. She moves about the classroom "living room," leaning in and listening to students engaged in the writing process, with honest and deep interest in their words and ideas.

Three girls—Hannah, Emily, and Ash—sit together in a small group, where they are working on a collaborative project. Today, their writing, their creating, stems from the article that they have just read and discussed with Mrs. Alexander and their classmates on the living room carpet. Fueled by the actions of the global women's march, they concentrate on the design of protest signs. Using markers, they discuss with each other the design of their protest sign and the message they wish to share. They use a hole punch to create a place to thread yarn so that their signs can be worn on the torso of their bodies. After ten minutes, their signs are finished. In large letters, their signs read: "Girls." Below the large print is the hashtag: #WhyCan'tWe?

Mrs. Alexander immediately responds to their collective work. Her eyes wide, she asks to take a picture of what they have collaboratively created. She responds to their intentional use of the word "Girls" being central to their protest sign. As young girls, they see themselves as part of a moment, a movement that their foremothers have started, and want to be involved in their own way. They use the discussions they engaged in during the morning meeting and "Read, Write, and Draw" time—the sacred time that is both routine and ceremony—to intentionally create their demonstration posters. They use images from the women's movement article to create and amplify their voices.

FIGURE 2.5. Photo: Hannah, Emily, and Ash's Protest Signs

On that same day, the girls take their signs and move toward public action. While the class is on the outdoor track on the school's playground, they begin to march. Together, they march and shout: "Girls! Girls! Girls!" In that moment, these three young girls enacted an activist stance by making protest signs and marching around the school's track. As they march and chant, and laugh, and amplify their voices, their peers curiously look on *and* listen. Other girls see them and join the protest, chanting to join in the raising of their voices in solidarity.

In Mrs. Alexander's classroom, we see the intentional ways in which she organizes the physical classroom space and time throughout the day to provide her students with the conditions necessary to engage in the practices of writers. Writing is taught as a content area, and it fills the spaces of the day, with students using writing as a tool to learn, to reflect, to examine, to critique, and to protest. As the lead learner and teacher, Mrs. Alexander truly believes that all her students are writers and encourages the many projects that they take up in their writing. This is evident in all the instructional choices that she makes with and for her students.

The morning meeting that we observe in Mrs. Alexander's class provides her students with time and space (Graves, 1994; Fletcher & Portalupi, 2001) to begin their day in community as writers. The ceremony they have created around this time offers students a consistent amount of time each day for writing and creating. In this meeting, and throughout the day, students are encouraged to take up writing projects that are relevant to their lives and that truly matter to them. Students have the tools that writers need and use readily available to them, and they are trusted as writers to make authorly decisions. Mrs. Alexander supports this work by drawing upon literature and text, both print and digital, that speak directly to students' lives and realities. Her students have autonomy and agency in the projects they take up, and we see how three young girls drew upon these resources to create writing that mattered to them.

The Importance of Physical Space for Writers

Ms. Bustos and Mrs. Alexander envision a physical space for their students in which they can grow as writers, discover their process, and share their voices and stories. In both classrooms, the arrangement of furniture, the open, flexible space, the vibrant colors, and the written work of students and published authors create an environment that is warm and welcoming. The space supports dialogue and collaborative work that encourages students to work through their ideas as they write. Across these spaces, Ms. Bustos and Mrs. Alexander intentionally place love in all aspects of the physical space, and it is both visible and felt.

The material culture of these classrooms communicates that these are places where real writing happens and where writers come to thrive. Around the room, the tools that writers use are visible and accessible to all students. They have books, pencils, markers, paper, and more at their fingertips to support their many writing projects. The voice of each young writer is present in every single space around the room through the personal art and published writing displayed on the classroom walls. Additionally, their thinking and growth is documented on anchor charts that are placed around the room as reminders of their work.

In these writing classrooms, there are clear routines for writing and sharing that foster dialogue and collaboration amongst all students. The students know that they have dedicated time each day to write. They come to their writing eager to participate and ready with their own respective projects. Both teachers search for literature and texts for their classroom libraries that provide mirrors (Bishop, 1990) for the many voices and perspectives that are present in their learning communities. These books serve different purposes in their classroom, and we see in their portraits the ways in which teachers draw upon them as mentor texts to invite their students into personal writing—"writing that matters" (Ghiso, 2011). Ms. Bustos and Mrs. Alexander masterfully use these books as a vehicle to connect to students' lived realities, showing the endless possibilities of sharing their perspectives and their stories in and beyond the walls of the classroom.

Pause, Reflect & Write

- In your educational context, can you map out the critical components for cultivating a writing classroom community? Is there ceremony? Is there a ten-minute time frame to "Read, Write, and Draw"?

- What did you notice about the intentional layout of Ms. Bustos's and Mrs. Alexander's classroom spaces? How did their design foster dialogue and collaboration in writing?

- Sketch the layout of your classroom space. Include furniture, bookshelves, student materials, and fixtures you cannot move (e.g., the whiteboard and the door). What do you notice? What changes might you make to foster dialogue and collaboration in writing?

- Think about the current sociopolitical context. What texts could you select to foster dialogue around the issues directly affecting students and the community? How might you create authentic writing around these topics?

Becoming a Bilingual Family of Writers at School: Contextualizing Writing for Many Purposes and Audiences

*I*n the first two chapters, we suggested that teachers of young writers design and enact writing instruction that begins with their students' cultural, linguistic, and familial resources (Moll et al., 1992; Gonzalez, et al., 2005; Yosso, 2005). Teaching vignettes illuminated the connections between time, space, and the material culture of the classroom in designing the conditions for developing the craft and voices of our young writers. We further suggested that teachers of young writers intentionally center students' interests and voices to extend writing beyond the classroom walls. By planning for ways to harness young writers' interests, teachers can expect the walls of school buildings to stretch far beyond their physical boundaries so that their young writers' ideas, understandings, hopes, and dreams may soar. For speech and writing in a bilingual classroom, teachers should value, embrace, and build on each student's rich linguistic repertoire within the English language and across named languages such as English and Spanish.

In this chapter, we present two bilingual teachers who organize their teaching of writing in the language arts with themes or projects that are mindful of content in and across other subject areas, such as social studies or science. Both teachers that we highlight are cognizant that "writing grows out of many purposes," as stated in the NCTE position statement on *Professional Knowledge for the Teaching of Writing* (2016). Instead of narrowing students' experiences of writing in school to discrete skills, these teachers provide themes and projects that allow for varied writing practices and activities that contextualize purpose, audience, place, and situation. Because the conventions of a specific genre vary, students are exposed to, provided practice in, and encouraged to reflect on the purposes and audiences of their writing in the genre they choose. In the following sections, we introduce you to Mrs. Ortiz, a second-grade teacher, and Mrs. Springer, a third-grade teacher. They each design particular projects or themes that expand the purposes of writing for their students. For example, to communicate with family members, young writers take on a translanguaging stance, by bringing in letters, drawings, emails, and other writings in the two or more named languages they possess. Bilingualism, then, normalizes translingual speaking and writing and draws on the strengths of being bilingual (Espinosa and Ascenci-Moreno, 2021; Piña, et al., 2015). To support young writers' expression of their linguistically diverse experiences, Mrs. Ortiz and Mrs. Springer intentionally cultivate a translanguaging stance during all aspects of writing instruction.

Mrs. Ortiz

> *Yo le enseño a cada uno de mis alumnos y sus familias a sentirse orgullosos de sus raíces y su identidad!* Together we grow, learn to believe, and learn to dream big!
>
> —Mrs. Miriam Ortiz

As a second-grade bilingual teacher in Central Texas, Mrs. Ortiz has some common linguistic, cultural, and geographical experiences akin to the experiences of her majority Latinx students. She grew up as the Mexican American child of migrant workers in the borderlands region of the United States and México. Although not all her childhood teachers recognized the value of growing up in a Spanish-speaking home, today she lets anyone who walks into her classroom know that "to be able to communicate and express our thoughts and feelings in two different languages adds value to our identity."

For her, language acquisition was a simultaneous rather than a sequential experience. In other words, she developed her language skills in Spanish and English simultaneously, side by side, rather than learning one language first and then the other sequentially. As a result, translanguaging across Spanish and English was an ordinary phenomenon in her neighborhood and community. However, the strict separation between the languages was promoted in her own K–12 schooling experiences, and "code switching" between named languages was seen as incorrect or inappropriate. Consequently, she trained herself to avoid participating in dynamic linguistic practices as much as possible, even with close friends.

Emergent Bilingual

Like Julia López-Robertson (2021) and many other bilingual scholars, we use the term *emergent bilingual* (EB) because it refers to children's "evolving bilingualism" (García, Kleifgen & Falchi, 2008). With this stance, the terms *English language learner* (ELL) or *English learner* (EL), which places English in the sole and primary position of language legitimacy, is avoided. Instead, researchers and teacher educators have talked back to policies that privilege English over the home language of students by applying the term *emerging bilingual* to such students (e.g., Tellez, 1998; Garcia, Kleifgen & Falchi, 2008; Garcia & Kleifgen, 2010; and others).

Code Switching and Translanguaging

Code switching refers to switching back and forth between named languages such as Spanish and English. Sometimes, it is called code-mixing. Each language is regarded as separate and autonomous, and bilinguals are seen as two monolinguals in one person (García, Ibarra Johnson & Seltzer, 2017). Translanguaging, however, refers to the complex ways bi/multilinguals use their *full bilingual repertoires*. Translanguaging goes beyond named languages (Li Wei, 2011) and refers to bi/multilinguals' creative use of interrelated language features from two or more named languages.

After ten years as a bilingual teacher, Mrs. Ortiz recalls, "If only I knew back then, what I know now, my self-esteem would have been higher. This code switching thing is actually an ability—talent—that requires higher-level thinking and that not just anyone can use in a conversation. I now proudly speak in two languages at the same time whenever I can." Thus, the shift over time of her teaching philosophy embraced emergent bilingual students' range of dynamic bilingual languaging practices of listening and responding orally and in writing between and among named languages. One day, she proclaimed to us, "I teach each one of my students and their families to feel proud of their roots and their identity!" This is a direct reference to her acceptance of flexible language practices in her instruction, now referred to as translanguaging. It is no wonder that in 2018–19, she was recognized as Teacher of the Year in her school precisely because she challenges herself and others in her life to write their stories and give flight to their personal and collective dreams using their full bilingual linguistic repertoires.

Creating a Community of Writers: "We Become a Family and Trust One Another"

One of the most important writing projects in Mrs. Ortiz's classroom is the creation of individual books authored by each student and celebrated with each other and their families at the culmination of the fall semester. Each child's book includes unique characteristics of their country of origin, specific family traditions, one family recipe, and a reflection about what makes their family special. The books and a traditional dish are presented as a *plática entre familia*, a family conversation, where according to Mrs. Ortiz, the family refers to the whole class and "we laugh, we cry, and we learn from each other" and from each other's experiences. This project, a second-grade portrait of a bilingual community, known as *Mis Raíces/My Roots*, aligns with and is illustrative of the NCTE position statement on *Professional Knowledge for the Teaching of Writing* that acknowledges the importance of creating "a sense of community and personal safety in the classroom, so that students are willing to write and collaborate freely and at length."

While this project is a tangible reminder of what a true classroom community can look like, it doesn't simply emerge out of nowhere. Rather, it is the culmination of a carefully crafted and curated year-long plan that places students and families at the center of the curriculum.

Mrs. Ortiz begins each academic year with the project *Héroes Latinos/Latino Heroes.* The purpose is to learn about notable contributions of Latinx members in their local and national community. Reading, discussing, and writing about Latinx heroes in September coincides with Hispanic Heritage Month and flows into October, when another project is launched. In *Cartas y Calaveritas para Día de los Muertos/Letters and Funny Poems for Day of the Dead,* the second graders are provided multiple opportunities to hear and respond orally and in writing to fictional and nonfictional mentor texts that are complemented by poems to celebrate Day of the Dead traditions. Mentor text selections can include *Just a Minute: A Trickster Tale and Counting Book* (Morales, 2016), *Just One Itsy Bitsy Little Bite/Sólo Una Mordidita Chiquitita* (Garza, 2018), *Pablo Remembers the Fiesta of the Day of the Dead* (Ancona, 1993), *The Spirit of Tío Fernando/ El espíritu de Tío Fernando* (Levy, 1995), among others. Then, in November, the classroom community of writers moves to the study of memoirs in the book project titled *Mis Raíces/My Roots*.

Each project links reading and writing, culturally relevant interests and mentor texts, language arts and social studies or science standards, and students' inquiries and families' funds of knowledge. The projects build on one another, each serving as a bridge into the next. Across these projects, students are exposed to mentor texts intentionally selected by Mrs. Ortiz and are invited to share what they notice in these texts. Their noticings include format features such as headings, photographs, captions, maps, and a variety of typographic features (such as fonts and the bolding of words and phrases) as well as the languages in which the words and story events occur. The second graders are asked to specifically note how authors use key words, organize their ideas, and illustrate their stories. Mrs. Ortiz shared with us that the "*Mis Raíces* project lends itself perfectly to embrace culture and to celebrate diversity. It empowers students and their families, as it is a take-home project where they collaborate in the making of a beautiful book that tells their story. This student-authored book focuses on their family's country of origin and what it's known for, their traditions, one family recipe, and a reflection about what makes their family special." Mrs. Ortiz loves how parents travel back in time and often share forgotten memories with their children.

In the *Mis Raíces/My Roots* unit, the students study and imitate content features of mentor texts about Latinx heroes and make connections between the heroic qualities exemplified by characters across the texts. They even notice how these heroic qualities also exist among members of their own families. The specific objective of the *Mis Raíces/My Roots* project, then, is for students to notice and use writing to express their own memories, experiences, inquiries, and events, as well as those of members in their families. When the sharing with parents and key adults takes place at the end of the semester, Mrs. Ortiz reports, "Our hearts pound together as I see all parents making connections with each other's stories. . . . *Mis Raíces* reminds us that we are different but similar."

In Figure 3.1, you can see a page from a student's book that showcases how he organized text and illustrations of his family, who migrated from Luvianos, México. This page demonstrates the thinking this second grader considered to communicate to his family and members of his writing community the elements and conventions of the autobiographical writing genre presented in book format. It demonstrates how

FIGURE 3.1. My Roots in Luvianos, México

¡Mis Raíces! My Roots!

<u>Translation:</u> *My parents are from Luvianos, State of Mexico and my grandparents are also. The town of Luvianos is picturesque, calm and full of beautiful traditions and customs. It is very special because the people are nice and friendly. The climate is very agreeable. There is no air conditioning.*

the teacher's and child author's purposes for writing both grew and aligned in the *Mis Raíces* project.

Building and Expanding a Mental Model of a Genre: Acrostic Poems

After the winter break, Mrs. Ortiz designs learning around a new project, *Más Allá de Mí/Beyond Ourselves.* In this project, students notice rhyme and figurative language as they listen to and discuss two mentor texts, *I Am René The Boy/Yo Soy René el Niño* (2005) and *René Has Two Last Names/René Tiene Dos Apellidos* (2009), both written as dual-language books by bilingual teacher and author René Colato Laínez. With a culturally responsive approach and triggering students' background knowledge about their family roots and what they learned through previous writing undertakings, this project continues and sustains the bilingual community's goal of instilling pride and uplifting individual and collective identities through discussion and writing.

In the following example, Mrs. Ortiz explains her process in teaching writing—in this case, acrostic poems. After reading the two dual-language mentor texts by Laínez across two days of Spanish language arts in her second-grade classroom, she recalls saying and doing the following.

Mrs. Ortiz:	*¿Les gustaría escribir un poema acrostico con sus nombres, como hizo René?*
	Would you like to write an acrostic poem with your names, like René did? [Students cheered and raised their hands with eagerness to begin writing.]
Santi:	*¿Pero que significa acrostico? ¿Cómo, maestra?*
	But what does acrostic mean? What, teacher?
Mrs. Ortiz:	*Les mostraré un ejemplo con mi nombre. Cada letra de mi nombre representa algo en mi vida—algo importante, algo que me hace feliz* and describes things I like.
	I will show you an example with my name. Each letter in my name represents something in my life—something important, something that makes me happy and describes the things I like.

As the teacher describes the writing assignment of creating an acrostic poem, she offers to use her name and reveal the experiences important to her as the mentor text. Mrs. Ortiz recounts, "I write my name from top to bottom on a blank anchor chart and add a couple of questions on the right side. I explain that I must think of as many important things about my life that begin with each letter of my name, and I must always refer back to these questions to help myself think of important words, not just any words. These questions are:

- Who am I?

- Where do I come from?

- What makes me happy?

- What are my dreams?

- Who or what inspires me?

- Who or what matters the most in my life?"

As she plans and enacts her mini-lessons to explain the process that leads to a piece of writing, she constantly models by asking and answering the key questions out loud for her students. She says, "*¿Quién soy?*/Who am I?" Then, she writes and says aloud:

| Mrs. Ortiz: | *Soy madre, soy maestra, estas palabras empiezan con las letras de mi nombre, la letra "M." Pero también me recuerda el nombre de mi madre, María. Ella es la persona que me inspira a ser valiente.* The letter "A" in my name *me recuerda a mi hijo Alfredito, quien amo con la fuerza del sol y de los mares.* |
| | I am mother, *maestra*, these words begin with the letters of my name, the letter "M." But I also remember my mother's name, María. She is the person who inspires me to be brave. The letter "A" |

in my name reminds me of my son, Alfredito, whom I love with all
the strength of the sun and the oceans.

Arli: *¡Hay maestra, que bonito! Eso es una metáfora.*
Oh, *maestra,* how beautiful! That is a metaphor.

Mrs. Ortiz: *¡Muy Buena observación, Arli! ¡Me da mucha emoción que lo notaste!*
We can all write metaphors like René *y como yo lo acabo de hacer.*
What a great observation, Arli! It touches me that you noticed it!
We can all write metaphors like René and like I just did.

As Mrs. Ortiz chooses the important words and experiences that describe
each letter of her name, she is intentional in her practice to think out loud and to
translanguage so her students know why the words she chooses are important. Through
her think-alouds about the words she chooses for her acrostic poem, and by moving
back and forth between English and Spanish, Mrs. Ortiz demonstrates how to make
connections to family roots, place of birth, her family, and what matters most.

Sofi: *Ah, ya entiendo. ¿Pero, también podemos escribir nuestros favorite colors
y comida favorita, como lo hizo René en su poema?*
Oh, I understand. But can we also write about our favorite colors
and favorite food, like René did in his poem?

Mrs. Ortiz: *Muy buena pregunta and connection with the book, Sofi. Claro que sí.
Las cosas que te gustan son parte de tu persona, de tu identidad.*
A very good question and connection with the book, Sofi. Of
course. The things you like are part of you, of your identity.

Leo: *Creo que ya estoy listo para empezar mi lista de palabras, maestra.
¿Podemos empezar ya?*
I think I'm ready to begin my list of words, *maestra.* Can we begin?

Mrs. Ortiz: *Claro que sí. Hoy solo haremos una lista de palabras. Recuerden que
tienen que pensar en estas preguntas. Los que terminen con la lista
pueden empezar sus oraciones en otra hoja. Les daré ejemplos de cómo
empezar sus oraciones.*
Of course. Today we will only make a list of words. Remember that
you need to think about these questions. Those who finish with the
list may begin their sentences on another piece of paper. I will give
examples of how to begin your sentences.

By showing the multiple considerations to be taken up by writers in the creation
of an acrostic poem, Mrs. Ortiz enacts what the NCTE position statement on
Professional Knowledge for the Teaching of Writing (2016) identifies as "a mental model
of the genre." She reads the two mentor texts and encourages students to notice ways to
recognize rhyme, metaphors, and figurative language. Understanding of the assignment

is aided when she models her own acrostic poem, making visible her own thinking to her students. Mrs Ortiz's writing also serves as a mentor text for students to draw on in their own writing as they organize their ideas. Her efforts result in students enthusiastically making their lists of words and writing their sentences, resulting in a much deeper kind of acrostic poem than those sometimes composed in schools. During the writing phase, she keeps the two mentor texts authored by René Colato Laínez readily available for her second graders. According to Serravallo (2017), it is a good idea to keep the mentor texts nearby at writing centers, for conferences or small groups, and sitting prominently on a ledge where students can easily pick them up or where teachers can readily use them for demonstrations (p. 26). On the other hand, the final draft of poetry is uniquely personal, explores what makes the authors feel strong and proud, and does not have to rhyme. An example of the writing produced in the study of acrostic poems is found in Figure 3.2.

Because in Mrs. Ortiz's classroom community the goal is to teach in ways where learners demonstrate their growth, not just in skills and content but also in their pride as bilingual, bicultural, and biliterate persons, she provides other thematic projects. While in the beginning of the academic year, she integrates the social studies standards

FIGURE 3.2. Acrostic Poem: My Name Makes Me Feel Very Proud

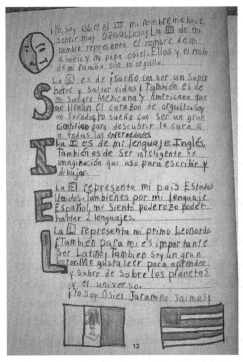

Translation: I am Osiel, III. My name makes me feel very proud. The O in my name represents my grandfather's and my father's name, Osiel. They and the rest of my family are my pride.

The S is my dream of being a superhero and save lives. It is also my Mexican American blood that fills my heart with pride. I am a dreamer. I dream in becoming a great scientist that cures all sickness.

The I is from my English language. It's also being intelligent and having imagination to use in writing and drawing.

The E represents my country, E.U (US). It is also for my Spanish language. I feel powerful speaking two languages.

The L represents my cousin Leonardo. Also, it is important to me to be Latino. I'm also a great reader. I like to read to learn and know about the planets and the universe. I am Osiel Jaramillo Jaimes!

with the language arts standards, in the second half of the year, science topics are integrated in the language arts. Some examples include *Leyendas del Sol y la Luna/ Legends about the Sun and the Moon, Plantas Ancestrales/Ancestral Plants,* and *Animales Prehistoricos/Prehistoric Animals.* No matter the cross-curricular topic she plans, the goal is for students to experience "projects that are authentic and student directed and that empower families by providing a platform that recognizes and embraces their stories."

Synthesizing Life in a Community of Learners

A student's artifact of writing and accompanying visual representation, like the one you just saw in Figure 3.2, can illuminate the portrait of the writing life of students in Mrs. Ortiz's second-grade classroom. It can demonstrate the purposeful guided instruction and a few of the experiences that students participate in across the year within the social context of their learning community. But Mrs. Ortiz goes even further in her work with young writers.

In Figure 3.3, the artifact is an illustrative case of another child's development in Mrs. Ortiz's class. This time, student writing shows the relationship between social activity across time and individual thinking about life after second grade.

The title *Mi Orgullo (My Pride)* signifies a key theme in Mrs. Ortiz's class that is evident in her educational philosophy as described earlier, in her classroom discourse with students, in Osiel's acrostic poem (Figure 3.2) and in Leo's essay about his pride and connection to heroes in his Latinx community (Figure 3.3)—i. e., Mrs. Ortiz, Ms. Martin, Duncan Tonatiuh, Leo Messi, and José Hernández. Interestingly, he used the title in English for Mrs. Ortiz instead of Sra. Ortiz and Ms. Martin instead of the conventional *Señorita* Martin.

The semiotic symbols that Leo uses are present both inside and outside of the thought bubbles that surround his smiling face. These symbols represent the connections he sees among his family, teachers, linguistic roots, reading, and love of soccer. This seven-year-old boy lets his community of writers know how impressed he is by the work of illustrator and author Duncan Tonatiuh. Leo is attracted to the specialized digital character included in Tonatiuh's many award-winning children's literature—books that include *Dear Primo: A Letter for My Cousin* (2010), *Pancho Rabbit and the Coyote* (2013), *Separate Is Never Equal, Esquivel! Space-Age Sound Artist* (2016), and *Funny Bones: Posada and His Day of the Dead Calavera* (2015), among others.

Tonatiuh is known for unique and beautiful illustrations and content that can be used for teaching in and responding to an anti-bias curriculum. In newscasts, he says he wants Latinx children to see themselves in books and to realize that their stories and their voices are important. These are the same reasons Mrs. Ortiz makes culturally relevant literature available to her second graders. She understands the importance of providing mirrors (Bishop, 1990) of the cultural traditions, histories, heroes, artists,

FIGURE 3.3. Leo's Essay on Pride

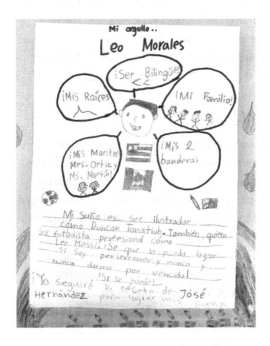

Translation:
My Pride ...
Being bilingual
My family
My 2 flags
My Teachers: Mrs.
Ortiz & Ms. Martin
My roots

My dream is to be
an illustrator like
Duncan Tonatiuh.
Also, I want to be a
professional soccer
player like Leo
Messi. I think I can
do it if I am
perseverant and
never give up!
Yes I can!
I will follow Jose
Hernández' recipe
to reach my
dreams.

conflicts, and contributions of the Latinx community. As a result of careful planning and exposure to culturally relevant literature and Latinx themes, Mrs. Ortiz facilitated Leo's declaration in Spanish that he dreams of being an illustrator like a member of his Latinx community, Tonatiuh.

Leo also reveals in his essay that he dreams of becoming a professional soccer player like Lionel Messi, considered by many to be the best soccer player in the world. The dual Argentinian-Spanish athlete plays soccer for the national team of Argentina. As a child, he overcame a growth-hormone deficiency, serving as an inspiration for youth like Leo in Texas and all around the globe. He is idolized for his perseverance, both on and off the soccer field. In his focus on Messi, Leo uses the perfect descriptor for a sports hero: perseverance. By going beyond simply the hero workshop to understanding the story behind the man, he accomplishes a rarity in young children's writing, whether learning to write in English, Spanish, or both. Thus, we can see how mentor texts that tell the stories of others can help students like Leo as they learn to write authentic descriptors about their personal heroes.

Another example that assisted Leo with his essay is the "recipe of José Hernández," which was promoted during this hero's visit to the school and remains available as a mentor text online. Former astronaut José Hernández was invited to speak at Leo's school, and his message was delivered to other schools in Texas and across the nation. Hernández reveals to children that NASA rejected him eleven times before he was invited to be part of the nineteenth class of astronauts. This message of not giving up is followed up by a recipe Hernández received from his father. The five-step recipe consists of:

1. Decide what you want to be in life.
2. Recognize how far you are from your goal.
3 Draw yourself a roadmap from where you are to where you want to go. That's going to show you the way and keep you focused.
4. Educate yourself. You've got to go to college.
5. Put your effort into your schoolwork, and then, when you get your job, put your effort there. Always, always give more than what people ask for.

Leo's dreams, as well as those of his peers in the class and school, are influenced by the personified mentor text that is Hernández and the recipe that has deep roots in the former astronaut's family, as well as other mentor texts that speak to his interests. These family connections in the stories read and responded to in Mrs. Ortiz's classroom uplift the value of interacting like family in classrooms and in students' homes.

The excitement, confidence, and pride that young writers in Mrs. Ortiz's class experience are shaped by opportunities she provides for students to study the format and organization of mentor texts, to study the choices made by authors and illustrators, and to invite linguistic and familial resources to writing productions. In this second-grade family of writers, the teacher also serves as a mentor text, revealing her own memories, feelings, thinking, and writing. Together, the teacher, students, and families build a community of writers that meets a wide variety of purposes for writing in and through named languages—in this case, Spanish and English.

Mrs. Springer

"A mentor text is the vehicle to explore our own realities, connect to the world, and validate our own experiences and richness."

—Mrs. Sandra Springer

Across town of the same Central Texas community, the type of bilingual family of writers that Mrs. Ortiz creates in her second-grade classroom is also emulated in Mrs. Springer's third-grade classroom. Both teachers have students who are predominantly of Mexican, Central American, and Caribbean descent. While Mrs. Ortiz is from the United States/México borderlands, Mrs. Springer moved to the United States from El Salvador.

Mrs. Springer completed an alternative bilingual education teacher certification program and a master's degree in curriculum and instruction with an emphasis on bilingual/bicultural education. Her own childhood in El Salvador was marked with the educational perspective espoused by Paulo Freire (1970), who believed education is not passive. Instead, he believed that education should be seen as problem-posing, reflective, and actively seeking freedom through voice and participation. Thus, for Mrs. Springer, teaching in her classroom is a recursive process of critically assessing the world to promote transformative learning. In her own words,

> I feel like I connect with Paulo Freire. He taught groups of adults to read the world, so that they can change it. To me that is very profound! He is one of the people who inspires me, because education does not just happen within these four walls. Right. Education goes beyond, and when you start teaching the kids how to understand their own situation, we hope that it is going to inspire them to take some action. Right. And that is . . . praxis . . . and his theory of the education of the oppressed.

For Mrs. Springer, this process of reading the world to change it includes reading culturally relevant texts with her majority Latinx students, writing responses to these texts, and taking action when an injustice demands innovation and change. At the beginning of the academic year, Mrs. Springer strives to learn about her students, their families, and their community, including the sociopolitical context where her students' families live. This is important to Mrs. Springer, as she seeks to integrate students' and families' experiences in her plans for instruction. She particularly "strives to move her students into a level of consciousness or action." She explains her recursive writing process in five steps:

- *Using community building and learning.* Every Monday morning, she holds a community circle, where the class has set up agreements that make the circle a safe place to share any of their personal, family, or community experiences. All class members contribute whatever they feel like sharing (e.g., visiting a flea market, the birth of a new family member, or the deportation or incarceration of a relative). During community circle, Mrs. Springer also shares about events that impact her own family.

- *Enacting informed teaching and learning practices.* Only after learning about her students' experiences does Mrs. Springer begin looking for the resources needed to connect learning in meaningful and contextualized ways. She looks out for and purchases culturally relevant texts that reflect her students' lived experiences. She is a tenacious researcher of websites, videos, and blogs (e.g., Teaching Tolerance, Edequity.com, Goodreads, Amazon, Cult of Pedagogy, librarians' networks, etc.).

- *Integrating content standards.* Guided by the Texas Knowledge and Skills (TEKS) to the theme she will be teaching, Mrs. Springer plans her academic goals. These goals typically include integrating reading, writing, and subject areas such as social studies, math, or science. For example, in teaching social studies during African American history month, she plans a unit on biographies that highlight Audrey Hendrix and Ruby Bridges. As young girls, these two biographical characters dared to challenge the injustices they experienced in their communities. Mrs. Springer uses modalities such as primary resources, videos, poems, and songs to deepen students' understandings within the theme.

- *Welcoming family and community experiences.* One vital element that helps her students understand and communicate through their writing is honoring their own personal, family, and community experiences. For example, when students learn about folktales, biographies, or traditions, she asks them to invite their parents to share their knowledge on these topics. She intentionally plans for the products of units to be tied to the families' funds of knowledge (González et al., 2005) and experiences.

- *Moving into action.* Mrs. Springer's ultimate goal is to further *concientizar* (raise critical consciousness) among her students and to move them into some kind of action in their community. For example, she guides them to see that "they have agency to change the things they dislike," such as racism, sexism, classism, or not caring about people, resources, and the environment. She wants them to be hopeful and to act upon their realities. For example, for a unit she named *Young up-standers,* some students placed posters around the school to prevent the trashing of their school. Others wrote speeches for a public meeting to prevent the closing of their school as rapid gentrification impacts their families and neighborhood.

Up-standers (Opposite of Bystanders)

For writing instruction, Mrs. Springer creates thematic writing work packets. Each packet has activities with elements of the author's language choices. For example, in her unit on *up-standers,* she begins by reading the mentor text *The Story of Ruby Bridges* by Robert Coles (1995) out loud, and then she and the students discuss it together. In their teacher-made writing packets, students have a diagram of historical fiction elements, which include setting, characters, plot/problem, and resolution as described in the real historical place and time of the mentor text. In the pages of the work packet, students are asked to respond in a variety of ways. For example, they are asked to respond to two photos in the book that are copies of primary documents. In the first, Ruby Bridges walks up the stairs of the all-white William Frantz Elementary School in Louisiana in

1960 escorted by four federal marshals. In the second photo, a white girl is seen holding a poster that states WE WANT TO KEEP OUR SCHOOL WHITE. Even though the event took place more than fifty-five years ago, the third-grade children in Texas express their feelings related to segregation and integration. One student transitioning from writing in Spanish to English responds to digitized black and white photos. She writes,

> *In picture #1 I would feel sad Because the girl is walking alone with 4 mans and with her frinds. In picturn #2 the girl only want whit pepol on the school and it is not fair that only pepol get to go and not Black pepol. Ther is a lot of white pepol and one girl Black.*

This student's writing shows approximations for English spelling based on phonemic awareness of Spanish and English. It also shows the young writer's inconsistent use of grammar understandings. For example, the consistent spelling of "pepol" keeps the vowels consistently making the same sound, like in Spanish; yet dipthongs require support, as Spanish does not typically use the dipthongs "ie" as in "friends" or "eo" as in "people." When "ie" is used in Spanish, such as in "quiero," the "i" and the "e" carry their own sound rather than the blended sound they make when combined in English. Also, the silent "e" in English is inconsistently used in the young writer's response in "white" and "whit"; this is also the case as is the sight word "picture," which is represented in conventional spelling, and "picturn." Because in Mrs. Springer's classroom, language approximations are normalized, the efforts of this young writer are accepted and treated as remarkable.

Other pages in the writer's packet include word study of expressions (e.g., *got by, get through, kept from, keep on, wear down*, and *hurried through*) found in the read-aloud and in the captions that accompany photos. Students are invited to find synonyms and antonyms, look up meanings and definitions, write sentences, draw pictures, or write the present and past tense of the expressions provided in the writer's packet. Mrs. Springer also provides students with direct quotations from the mentor text and space to write connections, inferences, and ideas. Students are expected to identify the fictional and nonfictional parts of the story. On one page of the packet, students practice summarizing. For the child described above who wrote about the two photos and is transitioning from Spanish to English, the summary response was:

> *Rubby Bridges she wanted to attend a white school. The white pepol didn't want her to go to school. But she stud up for herself and did not give up on what she belived. And the news grew en school. Became more integreded. Blacks and whit attended the same schools.*

As we saw previously, this student was consistent in her spelling approximation of "pepol" in both responses and inconsistent with the silent "e" in white. The dipthong in "believed" was missing, as it was in "friend" in the latter passage. Interestingly, in writing "stud up," the sound for "u" in Spanish is represented as well as the long "u" in English; at the same time, "up" was understood as a short "u" sound in English, a sound that does not exist in Spanish. In these writing responses, the teacher can assess the influence of phonology in approximated spellings and learn where students need further support.

After summarizing the content of the story, the students write about the ways Ruby's experiences connect to their lives. They think about and discuss with their teacher and each other the injustices they see happening today and what they can do to make a difference as an Up-stander. Across oral responses in class and written responses in their Up-stander packets, students identify that in their present day, they can go to school no matter the color of their skin. These topics of segregation, integration, and confronting racism were of particular interest to their lives because the school the students attended was slated to be closed. Historically, this specific school and community was majority Latinx, and gentrification was creeping closer to this rapidly growing downtown area, resulting in a controversial school district recommendation for closure.

Our transitioning Spanish-to-English writer stated at the end of her packet, "I know I can learn in white schools. I know I could make a diffrence" (spelling almost there!). Given that Ruby Bridges bravely stayed in the white school, this young child felt she could also make a difference whether she stayed in the school she now attended or had to move to another. For her, school was about learning and making a difference in the life of the classroom, no matter what the racial makeup.

Other classmates identified injustices that impacted them and actions that could be used to address them (see Table 3.1). The students brainstormed with their teacher and posed problems that impacted their young lives. They also discussed praxis, or actions, to support change to address these problems.

TABLE 3.1. Third Graders Problem Posting and Aligning Actions

Problems	Actions
Technology	Ask for whiteboards with touchscreens.
Deportations	Stop sending relatives back to their countries.
Fear of Deportation	Write to President Donald Trump asking that he stop deportations.
Homelessness	Give food and items for sleeping, such as carpets, money.
Raids	Speak out to express that immigrants want peace.
Bullies	Speak on stage about not bullying.
Recycling	Make signs all around school not to litter.

The five elements of the recursive process in Mrs. Springer's class, mentioned above, are practiced and repeated across the year. The students' writing and completed packets are tacked on the walls inside and outside of the classroom for all to read, ponder, and reflect upon. She used the same approach to teach (auto)biographies in a unit called Dreamers and Changers. This unit included read-alouds such as *Sonia Sotomayor: A Judge Grows in the Bronx /La Juez que Creció en el Bronx* by Jonah Winter (2009), *Brave Girl: Clara and the Shirtwaist Makers' Strike of 1909* by Michelle Markel (2013), and *Separate is Never Equal: Sylvia Mendez & Her Family's Fight for Desegregation* by Duncan Tonatiuh (2014).

The critical literacy that builds on practices to *concientizar* (raise critical consciousness) in young children results in many parents requesting that their child be placed in Mrs. Springer's classroom. For these parents, providing opportunities for their children to read and respond to literature with action regarding injustices in their lives assists them in raising sons and daughters that will be agentic up-standers wherever their futures take them.

As a teacher-activist, Mrs. Springer's stance toward education is a humanizing endeavor that stems from her own upbringing in El Salvador, Freirean education in her home country, and her lived experiences as a survivor of a twelve-year civil war. She draws upon her lived experiences and knowledge to create a curriculum in which she challenges her young writers to read beyond the words and see, act, and write about their world with raised consciousness about social problems. She designs and implements student centered projects such as Young up-standers. For this unit, she selected literature written about youth who worked to make a difference in their homes and communities through action. Mrs. Springer discussed the courageous acts of young protagonists in literature, highlighting the ways in which these young folks drew upon their many resources to take action and bring about change. From class readings, discussions, and writings, students in her class located problems in their school or community. The young writers problem-posed, designed solutions, and moved to action. Mrs. Springer supported her students in using their many cultural and linguistic resources through transformative language and literacy learning opportunities that extended beyond her classroom walls in truly empowering ways.

The Importance of Embedding Writing beyond the Walls of School

Together, the two elementary bilingual teachers described in this chapter embody the principle of writing as embedded in complex social relationships that bridge the classroom community (family), with students' families at home and in their communities. They acknowledge that power relationships are built into the writing expected from young composers. One of these power relationships rests in the choice provided to young learners regarding the named language in which to express their voice and the flexibility provided as they transition to fluency and competency from Spanish into English. Mrs. Ortiz and Mrs. Springer not only offer opportunities for students to grow in their understanding of features of good writing including phonology, grammar, and spelling approximations, but they provide projects, mentor texts, and varied modalities that deepen writing products created for different purposes and audiences.

Both teachers encourage the young learners in their classrooms to read the teacher's own personhood as a text. As we described, Mrs. Ortiz shares the stories and experiences that emanate from her name represented as an acrostic poem, and Mrs. Springer participates in classroom community circles. Alongside their young writers, these teachers share their own experiences and perspectives, offering a lens into their lives and ways to bring their concerns into action. In these writing communities, composing is familial and communal and is strengthened by all voices and ideas, in the classroom and beyond.

Pause, Write & Reflect
- **To what degree are students in my classroom family encouraged to express writing in transmodal and translingual ways?**
- **How can students' families be better integrated in writing instruction for the young learners in my classroom?**
- **What books mirror (Bishop, 1990) the cultural traditions, histories, heroes, artists, conflicts, and contributions of my students' families and communities?**
- **What books provide windows (Bishop, 1990) and sliding doors (Johnson, Koss & Martinez, 2018) to the worldviews of communities other than our own?**
- **What children's literature do you draw on to support the growth of young writers in problem-posing, reflection, and action?**
- **In what new ways can I capitalize on my emergent bilingual students' strengths and knowledge? (López-Robertson & Haney, 2016; Espinosa & Ascenzi-Moreno, 2021)**

Chapter Four

Leaning In, Listening, and Learning: The Transformative Power of Writing Conferences as Social Practice

*L*iteracy research conducted in writing classrooms has documented the collaborative, dynamic, and fluid nature of writing and learning to write (Flint & Rodriguez, 2013; Ghiso, 2011; Laman, 2014). In this research, classroom writing is viewed as a social practice (Street, 1995) that is not neutral and cannot be separated from the cultural context from which it is composed (Freeman & Freeman, 2006; Winn & Johnson, 2011). As highlighted in the previous chapters, time, space, culturally relevant mentor texts, teacher modeling, reading and writing connections, and continuous dialogue are critical components for writing instruction that tends to the social nature of writing. Educators who teach from this premise design a literacy curriculum that is centered on the lived experiences of their young writers; recognize the historical and sociopolitical aspects of their worlds; and base instruction in ways of knowing, being, and doing (Dutro & Haberl, 2018; Sinclair, 2019) as critical components of the learning and composing process.

One way that teachers plan for extended dialogue around writing is through individual and small-group writing conferences. The writing conference is a sacred time and space where writing teachers sit alongside their young writers, lean in, listen, and learn from their brilliance. During writing conferences, teachers take notes to document the composing processes of their writers and decide what writing strategies or skills to teach them in the moment to move their writing along for current and future writing projects. It is a space where relationships are strengthened, and young writers are nourished (Anderson, 2019).

The focus of the writing conference is on teaching the writer, not the writing (Calkins, 1994). Therefore, conferences not only support individual writing development but also serve as a springboard for the design of whole-class mini-lessons and future writing units that are based on the needs and concerns of the writers in the room. As described in the NCTE *Professional Knowledge for the Teaching of Writing* (2016), "When writers actually write, they think of things that they did not have in mind before they began writing. The act of writing generates ideas; writing can be an act of discovery" (2016). In this chapter, the stories we share of the young writers in the classrooms demonstrate their understanding of writing as a social practice. We show how they engage in authoring processes that are centered in their personal stories and situated within a larger social and historical context, thus adding important layers and dimensions to their words.

In this chapter, we welcome you to take a seat alongside two bilingual/dual-language classroom educators, Ms. Carmela Valdez and Ms. Sol Bautista, both teaching in K–5 neighborhood schools in Central Texas. Both teachers draw upon a writer's workshop (Calkins, 1994; Graves, 1983/2003) framework to organize their writing time and teach young writers. While their students are engaged in their individual writing projects, these teachers move around their room, pull up a chair, or find a place on the carpet alongside their young writers to conduct writing conferences (Hawkins, 2016). Through writing conferences, these teachers support their young writers in developing skills and strategies to add to their writer's toolbox (Bomer, 2010). These writing conferences also provide teachers with the opportunity for daily formative assessment of their young writers, offering a more holistic, full view of skills and strategies they employ across writing projects. The practices highlighted in each teaching portrait showcase the collaborative aspects that are integral to writing and teaching young writers. In these classrooms, writing instruction is contextualized, drawing upon the lived experiences of the young writers and those of their family and community.

First, we enter Ms. Valdez's first-grade, dual-language classroom, where her students are engaged in the writing of personal and familial journey stories. In this portrait, we see how Ms. Valdez used her kidwatching (Owocki & Goodman, 2002) skills during whole-group writing mini-lessons generally, and individual writing conferences specifically, to design a unit that reframed a new student as a writer and invited him into the writing community in powerful ways. During individual writing conferences, Ms. Valdez supports Roger through close observation of his composing process. She provides him with individualized instruction in concepts of print to support his writing from pictures to letters to words, in English and Spanish.

Writer's Toolbox

The resource for personal, creative, and powerful writing is the writer's toolbox. This toolbox can include special words and phrases and alliterative sentences the writer discovers, likes, and saves from stories, multimodal texts, characters in comics, and other diverse sources. A writer's toolbox is an individualized resource for personal, creative, and powerful writing. While the component parts may vary, teachers can set up student boxes to include the following:

- a space for wrters to note special words, phrases, or alliterative sentences that they've discovered and liked from the various texts they're reading.
- a place for writers to document their thinking about their own writing: prewriting, drafts, and reflections

A Writer's Toolbox can be digital and useful for organizing and tracking writing drafts. It's also a great source for talking or conferencing with others. Digital tools and platforms can help organize and track writing drafts. The writer's notebook is key for keeping thinking documented. Talking or conferencing with a partner at home and/or school about ideas in the writer's notebook is key to the writing process. See Bomer (2010) for more ideas. Additionally, Espinosa and Ascenzi-Moreno (2021) provide a plethora of ideas for writing tools in the bi/multilingual classroom.

Then, we join Ms. Bautista's fourth-grade, dual-language class, where her young writers are working on self-selected writing projects focused on a social justice issue that is of importance to their lives. Alongside Ms. Bautista, we witness the ways that she drew upon daily writing conferences to provide her young writers with individualized feedback to support their writing projects. Specifically, we zoom in on her daily conferences with Eric to observe how she offered advice and resources directly related to his work, connecting his passions to writing in powerful ways.

Ms. Valdez

I went to grad[uate] school and became an elementary teacher . . . to be the teacher that my parents never had but discovered that I would also be the teacher that I always wanted.

—Ms. Carmela Valdez

Ms. Valdez comes from a family of educators committed to children and families. Ms. Valdez was born and raised in the 1950s in South Texas, and her parents experienced prejudiceand linguistic racism in school. Her mother was punished for speaking Spanish in the classroom, and her father was not permitted to attend certain schools because he spoke Spanish. Their early educational experiences inflicted harm, causing internalized feelings of shame and guilt that impacted their identities. They became teachers to right this wrong they had endured and to ensure no other child experienced this same "linguistic violence" (Ek, et al., 2013) or, more succinctly, "linguistic terrorism" (Anzaldúa, 1987/1999).

Ms. Valdez's formal educational experiences started in a bilingual Catholic school, where her identity, culture, and language were celebrated, nurtured, and sustained. Her experiences changed when she entered an all-English public school. This is where she slowly began to lose her Spanish, as she was instructed entirely in English. This impacted her identity and the way that she viewed herself as a learner and as a Latina. Ms. Valdez describes the shame and pain she felt as a "hole that continued to grow in my heart."

Prior to becoming a classroom teacher, Ms. Valdez had a career in theater, during which she was a professional stage manager for more than ten years, working backstage at several professional regional theaters. After a while, Ms. Valdez recalls the desire to do more and knew that there were injustices in the world that theater could not fix. She enrolled at Texas State University, where she received a master's degree (M.Ed.) in early childhood education with a focus in bilingual education to become a certified bilingual elementary teacher. She says:

I found two-way dual language. It was a way to teach the kids who my parents were, English learners, and the kid I was, a heritage language learner. I relearned Spanish and began to find little pieces of myself along the way. I pick a little piece up every day that one of my students writes about what they love, discovers who they are in their language, and that they love to write because the best part of themselves comes out in the pictures and words on their page.

As a dual-language, bilingual first-grade teacher, Ms. Valdez identifies with the experiences of her students as they work toward bilingualism and biliteracy, and she draws upon her own lived experiences and those of her parents to be the teacher she wished for as a child.

All Students Are Writers & Storytellers

Ms. Valdez's writing instruction begins with the deep belief that every single one of her students is a writer and storyteller. She builds her writing instruction to center students' existing writing practices into her daily mini-lessons and individual writing conferences. Ms. Valdez knows that her students come from families and homes with rich oral storytelling traditions, which they engage in with their parents and elders as part of their daily lives (Leija & Fránquiz, 2020; Fránquiz, Leija & Garza, 2015; Reese, 2012). The stories that Latinx parents and elders orally share in Spanish and/or English with their children often recount memories from their own childhoods (Flores, 2019), family stories (Dworin, 2006), and stories of (im)migration (Gallo, 2017; Villenas, 2001).

Drawing upon this foundation, Ms. Valdez develops a writing curriculum that builds upon the storytelling traditions of her students. She explicitly names these knowledges and practices as valuable resources that good writers use in their writing and in sharing their stories. Ms. Valdez helps her students to discover that their lives are filled with stories—those passed along through oral storytelling and those that they experience in their everyday lives. She shows them that their experiences, both big and small, are worthy of writing and sharing with others.

For example, Ms. Valdez brings mentor texts into her writing instruction to teach her students how published authors and storytellers gather ideas for their stories from their own lives and experiences. One picture book that she reads and discusses with her students is *In My Family/En Mi Familia* written and illustrated by artist Carmen Lomas Garza (2001). In this book, Carmen Lomas Garza creates detailed illustrations that reflect her childhood memories growing up along the United States and México border in Kingsville, Texas. Her illustrations portray family memories, celebrations, and traditions. Alongside these colorful illustrations is a short vignette that further narrates the memory represented on each page. Through detailed illustrations and words, Carmen Lomas Garza provides a model for how writers and artists can use art and writing to share special memories from their lives.

In addition to this text, Ms. Valdez uses an array of culturally relevant picture books to teach writing strategies. Some texts that Ms. Valdez selects are: *Grandma's Records* (Velasquez, 2004); *Jabari Jumps* (Cornwall, 2017), and *My Papi Has a Motorcycle* (Quintero, 2019). These picture books support Ms. Valdez's young writers to "contextualize and situate their own language and experiences within the stories of other writers" (Newman, 2012, p. 25). Ms. Valdez also uses these picture books to provide her students with concrete examples of how they can compose stories based on their personal experiences.

Writing Conferences: The Heart of Writing Instruction

The heart of Ms. Valdez's writing instruction is daily writing conferences with her students. Daily writing conferences open space for her to lean in and listen to students talk about their writing. These ten minutes that she spends seated alongside a young writer open a window to learn about their process, see the strategies they are using as writers, and witness how they use images and words to make meaning of their lives and worlds. This is a space to teach her students strategies to move them forward in their writing and that they can draw upon across their writing and thinking.

For Ms. Valdez, writing conferences serve three important purposes: assessment, celebration, and advancement. As she listens to her young writers, she *assesses* where they are in their development as writers—the ways they are telling their stories, how they are using images and words, and what stories they are choosing to tell. Listening deeply to students read and discuss their writing, she then *celebrates* the beauty and brilliance of their words and ideas by intentionally naming these gems (Bomer, 2010), the beautiful, intellectual nuggets our students compose everyday. Finally, Ms. Valdez offers students a writing strategy or skill to *advance* their writing. Some strategies that Ms. Valdez teaches and reinforces are collecting ideas when students don't know what to write about (e.g., looking around the room, bouncing off literature, etc.), what to do when they think they are finished (e.g., adding more text or more details to illustrations), and how to add details. Ms. Valdez names the strategy, models it, and invites her writers to try it in their current and future writing projects. This is an asset-based approach, in which she begins with what they are doing as writers, naming and noticing what is there rather than focusing on what is not there.

The time that Ms. Valdez spends conferring with her young writers informs her daily writing instruction. Ms. Valdez monitors and adjusts her writing instruction based on the needs of her young writers. Writing conferences provide the time and space for Ms. Valdez to make the workshop varied and individualized for every student in her writing community.

Journey Stories

Based on writing conference notes and classroom observations, Ms. Valdez designed a unit of study focused on journey stories. The goal of this unit was for students to author personal stories about the many journeys they and their families have taken across time and space. For this unit, Ms. Valdez and her students broadly defined and wrote about their personal journeys and those of their ancestors. These included journeys to new schools, to new countries, and to visit relatives in different states. Through composing such journey stories, Ms. Valdez hoped to honor the journeys of her students as they reflected and remembered the courage present in these important, often unspoken histories.

To begin, Ms. Valdez introduced her students to two mentor texts, *Dreamers* (Morales, 2018) and *My Shoes and I* (Colato Laínez, 2019). In these books, authors compose personal journey stories with rich details and truth that speaks to the emotions and memories of their experiences. In *Dreamers/Soñadores*, Yuyi Morales recounts the journey that she and her infant son took from México to the United States. Although she left her family and friends behind, she brought so much with her—hopes, dreams, and stories. Similarly, in *My Shoes and I*, Rene Colato Laínez writes about his journey with his father, crossing three borders to get from El Salvador to the United States to reunite with his mother.

Together, Ms. Valdez and her students read and discussed both mentor texts, making connections across stories and to their own experiences. These stories highlighted for students the different ways in which writers use illustrations and words to compose personal stories. Their words invited students into reflection and examination of their own journey stories that they would compose and share with their fellow writers.

Small Pictures, Big Stories

Another important aspect of Ms. Valdez's daily conferences with her students is the personal relationships that she develops with them through the sharing of their writing. In particular, the writing conference became a sacred time and space for Ms. Valdez to develop a close relationship with Roger Moises, a new student from Honduras who joined her class. Roger Moises came to the United States with his mother to join family members already living in Austin. He had two names: At home, his mother called him Moises, and at school, he was called Roger. For Roger Moises, his names told different stories about the identities that he carried with him—the stories he would eventually compose.

Each day, as students moved into independent writing time, Ms. Valdez pulled up a seat alongside Roger Moises to confer with him. She observed his writing materials laid out in front of him. As he hunched over his writer's notebook, focused on the details of his drawing, Ms. Valdez asked, "What are you working on?" Roger Moises stopped what he was doing and moved his hands aside to show his drawing to her. Ms. Valdez smiled as she studied his drawing, nodding her head while taking it all in. Roger Moises had drawn a tiny picture representing his story. Ms. Valdez celebrated his drawing, asking questions to prompt him to add more details. In this moment, she let him know that she saw him *and* that he was a storyteller and writer.

In their daily writing conferences, Ms. Valdez, observed the ways in which Roger Moises came to share his writing and stories. Ms. Valdez recalls:

> He came to the United States very reluctant to put anything on paper. He worried that he would use the wrong letter to write something or that he didn't remember all the letters and their sounds. I made sure to explain to him that there was no reason for him not to tell his story. There were other ways. I wanted all my students to know that their stories were important, and they didn't have to wait for school to tell them what to write. What they lived and who they are is enough.

Ms. Valdez worked with Roger Moises and all her students to learn the importance of stories and the power of their words.

As Ms. Valdez gained the trust of Roger Moises, he began to open up more in his writing and storytelling, sharing more details about his life. Roger Moises took time each day to draw different parts of his story. In conferences, Roger Moises told Ms. Valdez intimate details about his journey story. He described the raft he took with his mother, and the van that met them when they reached land that drove them to the México border. He described the sweetness of the candy and Coke that were given to him while on this journey. And he told her about his feelings when he finally arrived at his new home in Austin and was reunited with his extended family.

As Roger Moises became more confident in sharing different parts of his journey story, Ms. Valdez introduced more writing strategies and skills to help him include letters and words with his drawings. One of the first strategies that Ms. Valdez named and reinforced with Roger Moises directly built upon the rich oral storytelling in which he engaged during his individual conferences. Ms. Valdez began recording their daily conferences to capture his oral storytelling and then invited him to listen to it and add more details to his pictures.

Ms. Valdez describes the ways in which Roger Moises's tiny pictures opened a window into his world and the complexities of his journey story. She states, "In Roger Moises's tiny pictures were huge acts of bravery, hope, and love." Through his tiny pictures and his oral storytelling, she learned about his life in Honduras, his family, and the journey he took with his mother to be reunited with their family in the United States. Ms. Valdez says that as he spoke, "the words that flowed from his mouth were like poetry." The books they read gave him permission to reflect and to explore his journey. Together, Ms. Valdez and Roger Moises engaged in daily storytelling, recording his words, which supported his growth as a storyteller and writer.

Observing this daily storytelling, Roger Moises's classmates became interested in the stories that he shared with Ms. Valdez. Slowly, students began to pull up chairs to lean in and listen to Roger Moises orally tell his journey story. Ms. Valdez said that at first, it made him feel anxious and nervous to have his classmates listen to his stories because he thought that they would think less of him. After one storytelling session, Ms. Valdez explicitly asked a student who was listening in if they thought less of Roger Moises now that they knew his story. The classmate answered enthusiastically, "No." She continued by asking, "Isn't that amazing, how brave he is?" She recalls an affirming head nod and a look of awe on the student's face. This made Roger Moises beam with pride in his journey and in his story, and it gave him the courage to continue to tell it and share it any way that he could.

This affirmation from his peer and from Ms. Valdez made Roger Moises more eager to learn the letter sound codes so that he could write words to accompany his drawings. Ms. Valdez worked with him to label parts of his picture, writing the sounds and letters that he could recognize to put words to the page to help to tell his story. She provided him with an alphabet chart to scaffold his letter-sound correspondence for sounding out words and recognizing spelling patterns. This was a resource that other students used in reading and writing that Ms. Valdez modeled how to use to support his writing. Roger Moises and Ms. Valdez continued to draw on these strategies in their daily conferences as he expanded the details of his journey story.

Ms. Valdez's work alongside Roger Moises is one example of the transformative power of writing conferences in her practice. She met Roger Moises where he was at, as a storyteller and writer, provided support, encouragement, and scaffolding to him. Through Ms. Valdez's directed and in-the-moment teaching, Roger Moises took his tiny pictures from drawings to oral storytelling to publication. In their conferences, and through bravely sharing with is classmates, Roger Moises became part of a supportive writing community that encouraged him in so many ways. Ms. Valdez expertly leaned in and listened to her students to learn about their lives and provide them with individualized teaching to move them forward as writers and storytellers.

Ms. Bautista

In the writing practice that I have created, I am always looking for what will be the most embracing way to develop a student's voice and identity as their most valuable resource.

—Ms. Soledad Bautista

Born and raised in México, Ms. Soledad Bautista grew up surrounded by her extended family in a small community close to the big, beautiful city of Guadalajara, Jalisco. Ms. Bautista's belief in the power of story and writing is rooted in how her parents raised her. Ms. Bautista points to her father's dedication to cultivating her voice and her mother's embodied lessons for always speaking her truth. Ms. Bautista's parents taught her from early on in life the importance of her voice. Ms. Bautista's parents also instilled in her a genuine curiosity about the world. They taught her to ask many questions and to evaluate the answers she received, then ask more questions. Ms. Bautista brings this valuable teaching from her parents into her classroom practice. She strives to center the voices of her students and the many languages and literacies they carry with them from their homes and communities (Moll et al., 1992; Yosso, 2005) into her writing instruction.

Prior to becoming a classroom teacher, Ms. Bautista was a psychologist. She became a psychologist because of her strong belief in the connection between the mind and the body. She spent five years working with adults and then transitioned to working with children with incarcerated parents. It was in this role that Ms. Bautista became fascinated by the idea of nurturing and transforming young minds.

Ms. Bautista was invited to enroll in a master's certification program with specialization in bilingual and bicultural education, with the possibility for cross-certification in the United States. This two-year program began in Guadalajara, where Ms. Bautista took theory, methods, and history courses. In her final year, she moved to San Marcos, Texas, to complete other program requirements and acquire her teaching certification. During that year, Ms. Baustista had her own second-grade classroom, where she drew upon her familial and cultural capital (Yosso, 2005) to teach reading and writing within a workshop framework.

Ms. Bautista has taught in bilingual/dual language classrooms in K–5 schools throughout San Marcos and Austin, Texas, for twelve years. She has worked as a teacher in the first, second, and fourth grades. As part of a dynamic and collaborative fourth-grade team, Ms. Bautista worked and planned alongside a team of teachers who drew upon the same theories and perspectives for teaching young writers and writing. Within this community, she found connections to her writing pedagogy and space to nurture and sustain her practice.

Social Justice Writing

Ms. Bautista designed a thematic unit of writing to invite her fourth-grade writers into exploration and examination of themselves, their community, and the world. For the unit, Ms. Bautista gathered a variety of picture books, digital stories, personal narratives, and other multimodal texts to open dialogue with students to inquire into their many identities. These materials were woven together to provide students with different entry points into composing a social justice-focused piece for publication. This publication would then be shared at a grade-level celebration of their writing.

To begin the unit, Ms. Bautista engaged her young writers in a class viewing and discussion of Chimamanda Ngozi Adiche's (2009) Tedx Talk, "The Danger of a

Single Story." In her talk, Adiche argues that "[t]he single story creates stereotypes, and the problem with stereotypes is not that they are untrue, but that they are incomplete. They make one story become the only story." Ms. Bautista and her students engaged in dialogue that centered the importance of moving beyond one reality—the one believed to be true—toward expanding worldviews to understand the realities and experiences of others. The fourth graders discussed the ways in which their identities influenced their worldviews and how learning from others can change them, helping them to grow as human beings.

Ms. Bautista also drew on personal stories from youth and adults through platforms like Story Corps, Youth Radio, and the Humans of New York. The stories and topics that Ms. Bautista selected were based on brainstorming sessions with students and were related to their specific interests. Some of the topics they explored included homelessness, hunger, immigration, racism, human rights, animal rights, LGBTQIA, Islamophobia, sexism, and bilingualism. Ms. Bautista prepared questions to focus her students' viewing of the videos and guide their discussions. Ms. Bautista's goal was for her students to understand how identities were formed and transformed through interactions with other human beings.

Ms. Bautista presented her students with three different stories from the Humans of New York, a photoblog and book collection of feature stories about everyday people from New York and around the world. One example focused on the story of a young homeless girl who wanted to go to school. This young girl enrolled in classes and found ways to save money so that she could continue pursuing her education. She shared that through this experience, she began to feel pride in her learning and all she accomplished. Once Ms. Bautista discussed these stories with her students, they each searched the site to read about different people and learn more about their identities and lives.

As Ms. Bautista and her students explored different themes related to identity, they gathered ideas in their writer's notebooks for possible topics to explore in their social justice writing. Each day after community discussions of read-alouds and videos, Ms. Baustista gave her students extended time and space to engage in quickwrites around their perspectives and emerging ideas related to their writing topics. Ms. Bautista's students spent a couple of weeks gathering their ideas and thinking through their different topics. During these first weeks of the unit, Ms. Bautista's writing conferences focused on helping her students talk through their ideas for selecting topics. For instance, one student was interested in writing about immigration, which is a very broad topic. Ms. Bautista engaged the student in conversation about this topic, asking questions and taking notes. She followed up the next day with more resources to help the student narrow their focus.

Alongside her students, Ms. Bautista wrote about her identity, and more specifically, about her evolving identity as she moved from Guadalajara to Texas.

Ms. Bautista shared the feelings and emotions she experienced as she explored Austin, explaining to students how some places felt safer to enter than others. She openly and honestly described the major adjustments she made to living life in English. Ms. Bautista's writing served as a model for her students. Through her writing and their continuous dialogue, Ms. Baustista made her writing process visible to her students. This supported them in making their authorly choices as they selected their topics for study and gathered resources to further their inquiries.

Ms. Bautista gave her students personal choice in the named language or languages they used for conveying their ideas in writing. She organized a specific conferring time with each student to discuss their writing, with a focus on language usage and audience. Each writer discussed with Ms. Bautista their very personal reasons for their language choices. Their choices were directly related to their own language identities and the desire for their parents to be able to read and understand their writing. Across all of Ms. Bautista's students, half of them composed their pieces in English, the other half composed in Spanish, and a few composed in English and Spanish.

Learning from Eric's Writing

Through daily writing conferences (Bomer, 2010), Ms. Bautista provides her young writers with the individualized time and space to enhance their craft and practice writing strategies. Ms. Bautista embraces the unique perspectives and experiences of her young writers. She believes that they each have distinct voices and styles that can further be developed through strategic writing instruction that is focused on their individual needs. For Ms. Bautista, conferences are a space where power dynamics shift, trust is cultivated, and relationships are strengthened. Ms. Bautista states:

> The power of conferring creates a bond between teacher and student that erases the roles and you become a pure source of knowledge-interchange and even though you have the responsibility to guide, you have the obligation to embrace freedom … Each student is unique in their style and in their needs. If they learn how to identify and verbalize their needs, they will become more independent in their work.

It is in daily conferring that Ms. Bautista learns deeply about her writers and where writing breakthroughs happen.

As the social justice writing unit progressed, Ms. Bautista's conferences focused on helping students gather resources for research on their topics. She supported them with the writing process through publication, specific to what they wanted to produce. Ms. Bautista confered daily, and for those with whom she did not meet face-to-face, she read their notebooks and left Post-It notes with comments, naming the gems in their work. The following day, she confered with these students to check in and see how their process developed.

One student, Eric, wanted to confer with Ms. Bautista every day. He would say to her, *"a mi no me gusta escribir cosas muy serias"* (I don't like to write about serious things), or *"no sé qué es un problema de justicia social que me afecte"* (I don't know of a social problem affecting me). Ms. Bautista explains,

> Eric arrived to fourth grade with a very strong writing identity. His biggest concern was his handwriting, as many other teachers from his past told him that he had illegible handwriting; therefore, he would never be a good writer. . . . He is a student with a strong identity and personality in all other matters, so it was very baffling to see him doubt himself in this regard.

Ms. Bautista noticed the concern that Eric felt as a writer and his belief in not having anything to offer through his writing and ideas. Eric loved fiction writing, comics, and superheroes. He had a remarkable imagination, which led him to create and talk about alternative plots to stories. Eric believed strongly in the "magic formula" to alter humanity's destiny and save it from destruction. However, he thought that since the fiction he loved was not "real" that his identity and what was important to him were not worthy for the unit.

Ms. Bautista conferred with Eric for several days in a row to discuss ideas for his social justice topic. Each day, Ms. Bautista searched for articles and videos to connect to one of the topics that Eric had collected in his notebook. Eric continued to express to Ms. Bautista that he was not going to be able to complete his writing because it was too difficult. Finally, after several days of meeting with him, Ms. Bautista told him that she needed to confer with other students, that she believed in him, and that she knew he would be able to write independently and find his topic. This upset Eric, and he went to his desk and sat down with tears in his eyes.

Ms. Bautista continued to confer with the different writers in the room. He waited patiently for Ms. Bautista to finish her conferences with other writers, and then motioned for her to come over to him. Holding up his notebook, he said, "Está bien

FIGURE 4.1. Visual of Eric's drawing.

así." Ms. Bautista read his writing and couldn't hold back her tears. Eric had written a masterpiece in which he had bundled all his passions into one social justice issue, giving life to a piece of protest and consciousness-building. Eric's writing was about gun control and mass shootings.

As a writer and designer, he did not want to include a title; instead, he chose to create a visual image to accompany his writing. Ms. Bautista celebrated Eric's writing, naming the gems and discussing with him how he might publish his powerful words for the celebration because his "writing was going to change some lives."

Ms. Bautista discussed different publishing options with Eric. He decided to publish his writing in Spanish and English. Ms. Bautista recalls:

> When finished, he wanted the art piece to be unique and powerful, like his writing. While we were brainstorming for his art piece, he told me, "What about the kids that don't speak Spanish? They won't be able to read this story that even made you and Ms. Thomas cry!" I answered, "I guess you need to write it in English, too."

Eric considered himself a "bad" English writer; however, the importance of giving access to his monolingual classmates and teachers was very high. Ms. Bautista spoke with Eric about how powerful it would be if he were the person who translated his own piece of writing so that his audience could grow exponentially. Ms. Bautista said, "I wanted him to finally acknowledge himself as a 'true bilingual' and for everyone to see his masterpiece." He agreed and began to write his piece in English, too.

These authorly decisions that Eric made about his composing process are highly intentional and intellectual in nature. Eric thought critically about his message and the many audiences that he wanted to reach. Eric's translations of his writing from English to Spanish is a sophisticated process in which he shifted his voice for a broader audience based on knowledge of his readers (Durán, 2017; Dworin, 2006; Martinez, 2010). Eric's composing processes and decisions were both celebrated and supported by Ms. Bautista, as she co-constructed the space with her writers and cultivated the conditions to nurture choice, voice, and language.

Making Writing Public

One of Ms. Bautista's writing goals for her young writers is making their writing public to show them the power of their words beyond the classroom. As part of the social justice writing unit of study, Ms. Bautista and her colleagues planned for the unit to culminate with a celebration of writing. Collectively, they wanted to ensure that their young writers had time to share their writing beyond the classroom and to engage in conversations with the community about their inquiries. Many of Ms. Bautista's students and their families had been part of the neighborhood and school community for generations, and it was crucial for them to receive recognition and love from the adults in their lives who had witnessed their growth.

Ms. Bautista and the fourth-grade teaching team collaborated with their students to plan and organize the writing celebration. Students designed personalized invitations to send to their families, and the teachers sent invitations to the school faculty and staff via the campus email. Along with these invitations, Ms. Bautista and her teammates made individual phone calls home to discuss the celebration and answer lingering questions. These invitations were written in English and Spanish and included details about the event and an option for guests to bring a dessert or dinner treat to share with everyone in a potluck. As Ms. Bautista notes, "food as a love language was very meaningful and important to many of our conversations around identity . . . it needed to be included as part of our celebration."

On the evening of the celebration, students displayed their final published writing on tables throughout the room. Alongside their published pieces, they placed blank pieces of paper for siblings, parents, and community members to leave compliments about their writing for them. This was a practice that students engaged in during their classroom writing celebrations with their peers and one that was an important part of honoring and celebrating the words and work of other writers. For each writer, this offered another opportunity to receive praise, questions, and feedback from the extended community—another audience beyond the classroom—to continue to move their writing forward.

As students arrived, they were greeted at the door by Ms. Bautista and her teammates. They entered the cafeteria, which had been transformed for the night. The lights had been dimmed to set the mood a la café poetry reading, with sounds of Latin music filling the air. Student writing was displayed on tables and around the different corners of the room. Lining the back of the room were long tables draped with large, colorful butcher paper in blues, oranges, and yellows, with vases of flowers on top of them. Families brought an array of antojitos, main dishes, and desserts to share and enjoy. This beautiful arrangement of homemade and store-bought food and drinks included a medley of fruit salads, street corn in *esquites, quesadillas, sopes, ceviche tacos,* hot dogs, sandwiches, cheesecake, strawberry *atoles,* and *ponche* sodas.

Ms. Bautista and her colleague opened the celebration by welcoming all families and community members to the event. They shared the goals of the social justice unit of study and the process they had co-designed with their students to research an issue of their choice and take through the writing process. In their welcome, they invited families and community members to first look at their child's writing and then walk around and view the writing of the other fourth-grade writers. They encouraged everyone to ask the writers questions about the topics they chose, which were related to their identities, and to provide feedback to the young writers.

After the welcome, families and community members enjoyed food, chatting, catching up, and some meeting for the very first time. Then, slowly, as people finished their food, they made their way around the room to read the work of each young writer.

One student, Yesika Torres, wrote about her life as an immigrant from México. According to Ms. Bautista, Yesika was very interested and engaged in the individual and class conversations related to identity. Meanwhile, Yesika had also just become a "big sister" and felt so much love, pride, and responsibility to support her family during these many transitions. She was eager and excited to share memories of her home and life in México. Yesika reflected on and shared with Ms. Bautista and her classmates how challenging the transition from México to the United States had been for her. She described the different foods, smells, and overall landscape of both countries. Yesika told stories about her family and friends and how much she missed them. She discussed the new sounds around her as everyone spoke in a language that she did not understand. These memories and feelings were reflected in her piece, *"Mi Vida Como Imigrante" (My Life as an Immigrant)*:

> *Yo soy Yesika, mi vida jamás será la misma a la de México porque no tengo familia aquí. No se siente lo mismo, el tener a toda tu familia en otro lugar, que tenerlos a tu lado todo el tiempo.*
>
> *Yo extraño mucho las sonrisas, los abrazos, la comida y todas las tradiciones que teníamos juntos en familia. Una tradición muy especial era Navidad, porque yo tenía ¡dos Navidades! Una era de la mamá de mi papá y la otra era de la mamá de mi mamá. En la de mi mamá, se reunía toda la familia y hacían tamales. En la de mi papa, se reunía toda la familia y compraban todos los ingredientes que iban a necesarios para cocinar. Hacíamos diferentes platillos cada año, todos ayudábamos a cocinar.*
>
> *Yo me vine a Texas a los seis años pero aún no se porque nos vinimos. Cuando me dijeron que íbamos a ir a Texas yo no dije nada. Ya que veníamos en camino yo venía llorando, pero después traté de olvidarme de eso. Cuando estábamos pasando la frontera yo estaba muy nerviosa de que nos dijeran algo y nos regresaran a México.*
>
> *Nos hicieron muchas preguntas como: ¿Porque quieren ir a Texas? ¿Por cuánto tiempo van a ir? ¿A donde van a llegar? Ya que pasamos la frontera no estaba tan nerviosa. Cuando llegamos a Austin todo era bonito casi como en México. Cuando llegamos vivíamos con los tíos de mi papá. Algunas veces íbamos de viaje a México y cuando regresamos de ir de visita, yo siempre lloraba. Todavía lloro mucho cuando les hablo por teléfono, los extraño.*
>
> *Yo se como se siente tener familia en otro país y no poder hablar o verlos todos los*

días. Me gustaría que las personas sean más conscientes de que el ser migrante es una cosa muy difícil. Mucha gente se burla y ve como menos a las personas por su color de piel, si son "legales" o no, por si hablan ingles o no. Nadie debería juzgar nunca a otra persona sin conocer su historia.

I am Yesika; my life here will not be the same as it was in Mexico because I do not have family here. It doesn't feel the same, having all of your family somewhere else, than having them by your side all the time.

I miss the smiles so much, the hugs, the food, and all the family traditions we had together. A very special tradition was Christmas, because I had two Christmases. One of them was from dad's mom and the other one was from my mom's mom. On my mom's side, all the family would gather together and make tamales. On my dad's side all the family would gather and would buy all the ingredients we needed to cook. We would make different dishes every year; we all helped with the cooking.

I came to Texas when I was six years old but I didn't know why we came. When I was told we were going to Texas I didn't say a thing. When we were on the road I was crying, but I later tried to forget about that. When we were crossing the border I was very nervous they would say something and deport us.

They asked us many questions like: "Why do you want to go to Texas? How long are you going to be there? Where are you staying?" After we crossed the border I wasn't so nervous. When we got to Austin everything was pretty almost like Mexico. When we arrived we lived with my dad's uncles. Sometimes we would travel to Mexico and when we returned from our visit, I always cried. I still cry a lot when I talk to them on the phone, I miss them.

I know what it feels like to have family in another country and not be able to talk to them or see them every day. I would like for people to be aware that being a migrant is a difficult thing. Many people mock us and see us as less because of the color of our skin, if we are "legal" or not, if we speak English or not. Nobody should judge a person without knowing their story.

Yesika's writing examines her deepest feelings and emotions about living as an (im)migrant in a new country. Her words speak to a longing for the people and memories that she left behind. She discusses the uncertainty of her life in a new country. Yesika's voice speaks directly to the hearts of other (im)migrants who may be experiencing similar feelings or emotions, while making clear that the journey and decision to move to a new country is difficult and that "nobody should judge a person without knowing their story."

This social-justice unit had spanned the entire school year and laid out around the room was the culmination of students' exploration and examination of themselves and their world. Ms. Bautista's young writers composed personal stories about immigration, family relationships, culture, gender identity, civil rights, and racism. Ms. Bautista's students developed identities as writers and expanded their repertories when they engaged in "real" writing (Dyson, 2020) that was rooted within their perspectives and worlds. In their writing, they drew upon their personal experiences to describe their feelings and the material realities of their lived conditions. As the community came together to read and celebrate each writer, the air was thick with feelings of pride and gratitude. Some parents were moved to tears, some read every single piece, and some stayed with one piece, letting each word and each thought composed by these young writers fill their spirits with hope and joy.

The Beauty of Our Stories

In Ms. Valdez's and Ms. Bautista's classrooms, we witness the ways in which these teachers build a writing community that fosters storytelling and draws upon the rich resources that their young writers bring to the classroom. During mini-lessons and individual conferences, both teachers model storytelling and encourage their students to draw on the literacy practices that are part of their lives. They invite students to share what they are already experts in—their memories and stories. Through oral storytelling, both Ms. Valdez and Ms. Bautista intentionally center the cultural and familial capital (Yosso, 2005) of their students, elevating these rich practices as an important part of their storytelling and writing community.

Like the teachers highlighted in the previous chapters, Ms. Valdez and Ms. Bautista use culturally relevant mentor texts in their writing instruction. They intentionally select texts that support their goals for developing and expanding students' writing and linguistic repertoires. The picture books they use to teach young writers strategies and skills also serve as windows into the lives of others and mirrors into their own experiences (Bishop, 1990). Teachers spend time reading and discussing mentor texts with their students to notice and name the craft moves that authors make and the ways that languaging is used to tell a story or teach a lesson. These books provide a lens for students to examine and share their experiences, as well as to affirm the richness of their languages, cultures, traditions, and personal experiences.

Finally, we see the way that Ms. Valdez and Ms. Bautista use writing conferences to provide students with individualized writing instruction to move them forward as writers. This is the space in which they leaned in and listened to young writers like

Roger Moises and Eric, to learn about them as human beings and as writers. For Ms. Valdez, her writing conferences with Roger Moises provided time and space for personal conversations and storytelling to flourish. Ms. Valdez's and Roger Moises's sacred conferring time helped them to build a trusting relationship in which Roger Moises found the courage to write his story and bring his tiny pictures to life. Ms. Baustista's writing conferences with Eric supported him in overcoming obstacles he had related to topic selection and his lack of confidence in his abilities to offer anything to the larger social justice conversations. Ms. Bautista and Eric used their conferences as a space to challenge each other to not give up, sending the message that they were in the work of composing—together. Through both teachers' conferences, their conferring practices illuminated how "the act of writing generates ideas; writing can be an act of discovery" (*Professional Knowledge*, 2016). Within their daily time together, Ms. Valdez and Ms. Bautista centered student voices, passions, and practices, encouraging their young writers to compose their stories, while naming the brilliance in their work. Ms. Valdez and Ms. Bautista started where Roger Moises and Eric were at as writers and storytellers and moved them forward by following their lead.

Pause, Reflect & Write
- **What role, if any, does conferencing play in your writing instruction?**
- **How do you organize your writing instruction to invite students to talk about their writing?**
- **How do you design writing units to center students' languages, cultures, and identities? What role can writing conferences play in those units?**
- **How can we make students writing public beyond the walls of the classroom?**

Teachers Amplifying Young Writer Voices: Inviting the Use of All Linguistic, Cultural, and Experiential Resources

O siel, a second-grade multilingual writer in Mrs. Oritz's learning community in Manor, Texas, designed this published piece of writing as part of the "*Mi Orgullo*" thematic reading and writing unit developed by his teacher and discussed in Chapter 3. In his published piece, Osiel describes what he carries with him, from his *raíces, familia*, and teacher who give him superpowers "*en el ring de la vida.*" With his words expressed through Spanish/English translanguaging, he has designed a super*heróe*, representing himself, as el "Rayo Flash" with a CH on his long red cape that signifies his nickname at home, "Chelito." This super*heróe* wears a red mask (a lucha libre mascara) complete with boots and hat (botas and sombrero) that express the *orgullo*, the pride, that Osiel feels in himself. Through images and words, Osiel creates writing that is personal and meaningful to him and his family.

As we learned in Chapter 3, during the school year, Mrs. Ortiz engaged her students in a contextualized and connected biographical and author's study of Latinx *heróes*. This study immersed Mrs. Ortiz's students in the lives of influential Latinx public figures like NASA Astronaut José M. Hernández and Supreme Court Justice Sonia Sotomayor and storytellers and children's book authors like René Colato Laínez, Yuyi

FIGURE 5.1. Osiel's Super*heróe* "El Rayo Flash"

Soy un luchador en el ring de la vida.
Mis raíces, mi familia, mi maestra Mrs. Ortiz
me dan el superpower para alcanzar las
estrellas
!Si Se Puede!

I am a fighter in the ring of life.
My roots, my family, my teacher Mrs. Ortiz
give me the superpower to reach the stars.
Yes, You Can!
—Osiel Jaramillo, second-grade
multilingual writer and super*heróe*

Morales, and Duncan Tonatiuh. Through continuous dialogue, Mrs. Ortiz and her students learned about the challenges these Latinx figures faced at the intersections of race, class, gender, and immigration status, while also illuminating their joy and success. The writing that Mrs. Ortiz's young writers composed as part of this learning was designed to extend their knowledge of the lives of these figures, while at the same time to give them a deeper understanding of their heritage and the funds of strength present in their own lives and their *raíces*.

This small snapshot of Osiel's writing tells a larger story of the work that Mrs. Ortiz and her second-grade multilingual writers accomplished throughout an entire school year. Osiel's writing is not part of one isolated thematic unit. His writing is part of Mrs. Ortiz's yearlong vision for developing biliteracy and bilingual language learning that is culturally responsive and connected to students and their families' lives. As Mrs. Ortiz states:

> My intention as an educator [is] to create an opportunity for my students
> to make a deeper connection with their own lives, to help them discover the
> meaning of inspiration, and to gain a deeper understanding of culture. The

work of these public figures and their achievements despite the obstacles they faced in their life journey to success inspire many of us to believe in our own dreams and instill pride in who we are and where we come from.

Cultivating Young Writers

Across these portraits of young writers, we have introduced you to six teachers in Arizona and Texas serving young writers and their families in K–5 classroom settings. Each teacher works in very different contexts across the southwestern region of the United States. These teachers work in English-only contexts and within schools and districts with bilingual and dual-language educational options. These contextual differences span cities, states, and school sites that are influenced by local and national educational policies and mandates. It is within these various sociocultural and sociopolitical contexts that these teachers serve students and families, and where we witness their commitment and love for their work alongside their young writers.

In Chapter Two, we entered Ms. Bustos's and Mrs. Alexander's classrooms, and we see the ways in which the arrangement of the material culture of their classroom community foregrounds the teaching and learning opportunities they design and facilitate for their young learners. The physical space is colorful, is filled with rugs and comfortable seating areas, and has all the tools that writers need to write their lifeworlds. The walls of each classroom are covered with their work, as writers, storytellers, artists, and inquirers, telling the story of their collective learning and thinking throughout the school year. Both Ms. Bustos and Mrs. Alexander work to create a classroom community that is warm and inviting for their students while making learning relevant to their everyday lives.

Through classroom arrangement and structured opportunities to share and listen to one another, Ms. Bustos and Mrs. Alexander seek to foster deep relationships between their students through which rich learning can happen. They arrange their time and space to facilitate dialogue and inquiry through and within writing. As the lead learners, they model, through their actions and words, how to lean in, listen, hold space, contribute, and learn within a community of writers. Together with their students, they have created important rituals and routines that support and lift the level of writing in the room. This is evidenced in Ms. Bustos's read-alouds and the ways she models her own thinking process and writing in front of her young writers. Her modeling is interactive and dialogic, inviting her students into conversation about her experiences and with each other, which highlights the social aspect of the writing process in their community. Mrs. Alexander's morning meetings serve as a ceremony in her learning community, with the goals of immersion into relevant literacy that builds on the funds of knowledge (Moll et al., 1992; González et al., 2005) from students' homes and experiences in the wider community. In this daily practice, we see how Mrs. Alexander's young writers take ownership in this predictable time of their day. This was highlighted specifically when three young writers used this space to engage in a movement happening locally and nationally to speak up and out for girls' and women's rights.

Throughout Chapter Three, Mrs. Oritz's and Mrs. Springer's curriculum and teaching practices illuminate their belief and vision that "writing grows out of many purposes." Both Mrs. Ortiz and Mrs. Springer work toward developing the consciousnesses of their young writers through engagement in reflection and examination of themselves, their families, and their world. They design reading and writing projects with themes that are contextualized and seamlessly connected to one another. In their teaching, they center students' cultural and linguistic resources to foster *orgullo*—pride—in their heritage as bilingual, bicultural, and biliterate children.

Within their curricula, Mrs. Ortiz and Mrs. Springer design opportunities to engage family and community knowledges and experiences through writing and across content areas. Mrs. Ortiz's yearlong curriculum offers many connected opportunities through reading, writing, and dialogue for her students to research and learn more about their family traditions and histories. In their collective work, Mrs. Ortiz's students discover more about their roots, their histories, and their own stories. Similarly, Mrs. Springer opens space to learn deeply about her students and their families, and the sociopolitical context in which they live, to design a curriculum that is rooted in their experiences. From this deep knowledge of her students and their families, Mrs. Springer designed the young Up-standers unit to study the lives of young people, both historically and contemporary, and how they used their voices to make a difference in their communities and the world. Through this work, Mrs. Springer and her young writers put their research and literacy into action advocating through writing and creating words for
change. These young voices, as well as the voices in Mrs. Ortiz's classroom, could be expressed in English, Spanish, or through both languages. In this way, evolving bilingualism (García, Kleifgen & Falchi, 2008) and biliteracy is embraced, and each student's rich linguistic and cultural repertoire is a resource that can be used in and for authoring.

In Chapter Four, you learned how Ms. Valdez and Ms. Bautista design their writing curriculum to support their young writers with many opportunities to learn about themselves and each other through writing and storytelling. Their teaching highlights the ways in which "the act of writing and [storytelling] can be an act of discovery" (*Professional Knowledge*, 2016). They structure their writing block using a writer's workshop framework. This provides Ms. Valdez and Ms. Bautista with pedagogical tools to support their young writers in writing on self-selected topics for extended amounts of time while they confer with individual students. As we witnessed in their portraits, the writing conference is the heart of their writing instruction, where they spend time daily with their young writers discussing individual writing projects, learning about their writing processes, and modeling strategies to move them along in their writing journeys. Ms. Valdez's work alongside Roger Moises and Ms. Bautista's work alongside Eric demonstrate how the writing conference can be a sacred space for dialogue that is individualized to nurture the voices and processes of each writer.

Both Ms. Valdez and Ms. Bautista model for their young writers the ways they draw upon their personal histories and stories from their childhood, family, and community in their own "real writing" (Dyson, 2020). This model opens rich conversations for their young writers to learn about their teachers in authentic ways while also opening space for them to examine and consider their histories and the stories embedded in their lived experiences. Ms. Valdez developed a unit of study to center the brave and courageous journey stories of her young writers, and specifically to reframe Roger Moises as a writer and privilege the important stories and knowledge he brought with him as a newcomer to the school and to the learning community. Ms. Bautista, along with her team, designed a yearlong interdisciplinary unit of study focused on identity and social justice that culminated in a community celebration of each young writer, making their writing public. Within this unit, Ms. Bautista used writing conferences to provide her young writer, Eric, with guidance about identifying a writing topic until she knew that he was ready to "fly solo" and put his passion on gun violence and goals of the unit into powerful writing in two named languages, English and Spanish.

Together, these classroom portraits highlight a vision for teaching young writers and designing a writing curriculum that frames all students as brilliant writers and storytellers. This vision, as articulated in the NCTE position statement on *Professional Knowledge for the Teaching of Writing* (2016) states, "Everyone has the capacity to write; writing can be taught; and teachers can help students become better writers" (p. 9). The practices of these classroom teachers provide us with concrete tools to create writing classrooms that build on the linguistic, cultural, and experiential strengths and resources of each young writer in our learning communities.

Supporting Young Writers to Amplify Their Voices

Each classroom portrait showcased in this book provides an in-depth example of the work that six teachers engage in with their young writers. In their portraits, we saw overlapping practices and tools used to support their work with young writers in their classrooms. Their goals are to develop the craft of all their writers and guide them to recognize the power of their voices through writing for various purposes. In the next sections, we briefly discuss the practices and tools present in these writing communities and the ways in which they can be taken up by language arts teachers for all writers in K–5 classrooms.

Learning from Published Writers

The literature that teachers bring into their classrooms to facilitate craft lessons and model strategies during writing mini-lessons is supported by the works of published authors and storytellers who write from a variety of perspectives, languages, and purposes. Teachers select literature books and digital and multimodal texts to engage their young writers in the practices and processes of published writers as they learn to live "writerly lives." Additionally, these literature books and multimodal texts help teachers to demystify the writing process and support young writers in finding their own practices, processes, and purposes as writers.

In the classrooms portrayed in this book, teachers intentionally select mentor texts that are relevant and connect to learners' histories and lives. Teachers seek out fiction and nonfiction literature, as well as multimodal texts, from authors and storytellers whose voices and experiences represent a wide range of perspectives and linguistic practices. Throughout these classrooms, we see the selection of many diverse writers and storytellers presented in mini-lessons and read-alouds to teach language art skills and strategies. These classroom stories highlight the ways in which writers draw upon their own lives and experiences for inspiration in writing. These texts serve as invitations for young writers to examine their own histories, alongside those of published writers and storytellers (López, Ynostroza, Fránquiz & Curiel, 2015). They provide models for young writers to imagine the possibilities of the stories that exist in their own lives and the importance of remembering and representing the recollections in drawing, writing, and/or multimodal expressions.

Centering the Lived Experiences of Young Writers

Through their "writerly stance" (Di Pardo, Storms & Selland, 2011) and their classroom practices, we have witnessed how the six teachers highlighted in this book show young writers how to connect their personal identities at home and within the wider community with emergent social identities at school. These teachers design writing curricula that invites young writers to explore their family histories while also examining and interrogating the sociopolitical context of the then and now. The teachers' writing curricula also invites researching of social-justice issues in students' communities and the world. Coupled with reading and discussion of literature and multimodal texts, young writers are able to extend their understandings of their personal experiences and gain new insight into the historical and contemporary social-justice issues that matter most in their lives.

Young writers in these classroom portraits were encouraged to author personal stories from their lives and compose writing that challenged sociopolitical contexts impacting their lives or the lives of loved ones. Like Lewison and Hefferman (2008) found in their third-grade study, the six teachers captured in this book worked with their students to gain an understanding of the power of their "writing as a way to get important work done in the world" (p. 438).   In these classrooms, young writers learned the power that their voices and words held as tools for advocacy when they repositioned themselves as agents for change.

Engaging Families in Writing

These portraits provide insight into how these teachers created opportunities for the families of their young writers to be engaged in the writing and learning that was occurring in the classroom. Teachers put a great deal of care and energy into learning and understanding students and their families' cultural, linguistic, and aspirational resources (Yosso, 2005). This is demonstrated through the routines and rituals embedded in the storytelling and sharing that occurred in community circles, morning meetings, mini-lessons, read-alouds, and individual conferences. These community rituals and routines opened space for deep sharing and conversations, as well as for composing personal stories about family, home, and community, and about personal and social issues that matter.

Teachers can draw upon this knowledge of students' lives and their families in the design of writing curriculum. The teachers highlighted developed units that included components for students to engage in discussions with their parents about their family histories and traditions (Alvarez, 2020; Flores & Springer, 2021; Leija & Fránquiz, 2020). They read about real heroes who transformed thinking about the world as we know it as well as outer space. These literacy practices allowed for families to be engaged in the learning without having to physically come to school, which can be difficult for parents who may work multiple jobs or have had negative experiences related to their own education (López-Robertson, 2017). Teachers also invited families to participate in writing celebrations to listen to and read the work published by their young writers.

Making Writing Public

In these classrooms, teachers provide multiple opportunities for young writers to make their writing public. During daily writing instruction, young writers share their writing in process with partners and in small groups to bring their stories and words into the classroom. This sharing offers all young writers the opportunity to hear the different stylistic and linguistic choices that their peers are making and in turn lifts the level of writing in the room as they "try on" different styles and strategies in their own writing.

Teachers hang student-produced writing around their classroom and throughout the hallways of their schools to put a spotlight on the work of their young writers. This display of writing celebrates student creativity and creates an atmosphere that values the learning, the voices, and the perspectives of each young writer. In the case of a young writer in Ms. Bautista's classroom, the process of living and writing in a community of writers studying issues of social justice are thoughtfully and confidently expressed by Abel in Spanish and available for the public to contemplate.

LGBTQQIAPD

Escrito por: Abel Sanchez Jasso

Yo voy a hablar de LGBTQQIAPD esta es una comunidad de personas que tienen diferente preferencia sexual. Pero aunque tienen diferente preferencia sexual no significa que tenemos que tratarlos diferente porque todos somos iguales, somos humanos. **Yo apoyo a las personas de esta comunidad aunque a las demás personas no les guste.** *La L significa lesbiana, la G significa gay, la B significa bisexual, la T significa transexual, la Q significa queer, la otra Q significa questioning (preguntándose), la I significa intersexual, la A significa asexual, la P pansexual y la D demisexual.*

Nadie debe juzgar a las demás personas solo por como se miran o de quien se enamoran, eso es muy injusto. A mi no me importa la preferencia sexual de nadie a mi lo único que me importa es que seas feliz. No pidas ni escuches las opiniones de los demás. Las diferencias son importante en el mundo porque por todos somos iguales por dentro. La felicidad es lo que más me importa, las diferencias nos hacen únicos y eso es muy bueno. Yo espero que al leer esto todos aprendan a no tener miedo de ser gay, lesbiana o transexual o lo que tu seas, lo más importante es ser feliz.

Translation: I am going to talk about LGBTQQIAPD this is a community of people who have different sexual preferences. But even if they have different sexual preferences, it does not mean that we treat them differently because we are all the same, we are human beings. **I support persons from this community even if other people do not like it.** The L means lesbian, the G means gay, the B means bisexual, the T means transsexual, the Q means queer, the other Q means questioning (questioning oneself), the I means intersexual, the A means asexual, the P pansexual and the D demisexual.

No one should judge other people only by their looks or with whom they
fall in love, that is very unjust. To me someone's sexual preference is not
important, for me the only thing is that the person is happy. Don't ask for
or listen to the opinions of others. In the world differences are important
because inside we are all the same. Happiness is what matters most to me,
the differences make us unique and that is great. I hope when others read
this they will not be afraid to be gay, lesbian or transsexual or whatever you
are, the most important thing is to be happy.

During the social-justice writing unit in Ms. Bautista's class, conferences focused on
helping students like Abel gather textual and multimodal resources for researching
their selected topic. She supports young writers with the space and time necessary to
take writing ideas from selection of topic to publication. As we have seen, this means
honoring routines such as conferring daily, reading drafts in student notebooks, leaving
sticky notes with comments, and naming the gems that brighten their work. As a
result, Axel learned about and took a stance for a community that has been historically
oppressed, stereotyped, and misunderstood. He writes confidently in Spanish for the
public to know that for him members, of all communities deserve to be happy.

Creating Visions for Cultivating Young Writers

*I wrote this piece because I believe it's my duty as a Mexican American to change
people's minds about Mexicans and stereotypes people say about them because I
believe that everyone is equal and everyone should be respected.*

—Virginia, fourth-grade writer

We end this book by circling back to Virginia, a fourth-grade writer in Ms. Bautista's
classroom in Austin, Texas. These are the final words in Virginia's published piece, "My
Mexican Culture," that she displayed for the school community to read on the night
of the celebration of writing. Her words illuminate the power of writing, to change
lives, to speak truth to power, and to transform the world. Through her words, Virginia
speaks to the role that she believes, as a Mexican American writer, is hers—to "change
people's minds." Through her writing, she speaks back to the falsehood of a single story
(Adiche, 2009). Instead, she writes about what it means to her to be a Mexican and a
Mexican American, the ways the beauty of her culture enriches stories learned from her
family and the truth that "everyone should be respected." Virginia knows she has taken

her writing from its inception to a published piece for herself *and* her community. She knows and celebrates that her words and her voice matter.

All the stories, perspectives, and brilliance of the young writers mentioned in this book were nurtured by their teachers. These teachers started with an asset view of each writer, framing them from the beginning as readers and writers. Each teacher created a curriculum for a different community that was uniquely contextualized, while providing intentional strategies to move students along in their writing journeys. The six teachers helped their students to see themselves as writers and to develop pride in who they are and who they are becoming. They believe that each child is a writer with a story to tell to change the world.

Pause, Reflect & Write
- **What is one practice that you might take up in your classroom? How would you modify it to meet the needs of your students?**
- **In what ways are the children in your classroom community drawing on their family's and community's funds of knowledge?**
- **How will you make writing public in your classroom and school community?**

Annotated Bibliography: Resources for Writing Teachers

Books

Baines, Janice, Carmen Tisdale, and Susi Long
"We've Been Doing It Your Way Long Enough": Choosing the Culturally Relevant Classroom
Teachers College Press, 2018

Written by and for educators, this book opens classroom spaces to illuminate decolonizing and humanizing culturally relevant literacy pedagogies that center the cultural, familial, and linguistic knowledges and practices of children, families, and communities. Janice Baines, Carmen Tisdale, and Susi Long offer strategies to support teachers in the examination of their classroom spaces and practices to begin to dismantle power and privilege within their own learning communities. The authors provide suggestions from their own practices for building relationships with families and communities, designing a curriculum that is rooted in students' lives, and for teaching within standards while also extending learning to critique and challenge oppressive systems. Oral histories, music, and storytelling are all at the center of classroom learning.

Bomer, Katherine
Hidden Gems: Naming and Teaching for the Brilliance in Every Student's Writing
Heinemann, 2010

Responding to writing and the writer is essential work that can be difficult at times. The book provides generative feedback to move the writer and writing forward. In *Hidden Gems*, Katherine Bomer provides protocols, language, and demonstrations to support writing teachers in responding to the brilliant writing that writers compose to help move them forward in powerful ways. Key to this work is teacher reflection and examination of our own experiences as writers, which Bomer invites us to engage in throughout the book. A masterful teacher of writers, Bomer teaches us to always center the writer, honor their craft, celebrate the smart things they do, and name them.

Buckner, Aimee
Notebook Know-How: Strategies for the Writer's Notebook
Stenhouse, 2005

The writer's notebook is at the heart of the writing life, where we teach our students to collect, gather, and document moments they never want to forget. There are many ways to keep a writer's notebook, and finding strategies and tools to add to our toolkits is vital to our work as writing teachers. In this book, Aimee Buckner describes how she uses the writer's notebook in her own classroom. She provides a variety of entry points, along with examples from her own teaching for getting students started, organizing them, and sustaining them throughout the school year.

Espinosa, Cecilia, and Laura Ascenzi-Moreno
Rooted in Strength: Using Translanguaging to Grow Multilingual Readers and Writers
Scholastic, 2021

At the core of this book are research-based experiences with emergent bi/multilingualism. It is based on translanguaging theory, which posits the idea that teachers and students flourish in educational settings where two or more named languages are valued. A rich presentation of instructional strategies for inviting and assessing each child's complete linguistic repertoire in speaking, listening, reading, and writing is at the root of this literacy approach. The strength of translanguaging and the materials and activities that can assist teachers in building the linguistic assets of their students is expertly presented for use in any classroom. Included are ideas for guided reading, shared reading, writer's workshops, and assessments for the language-centered classroom.

Fletcher, Ralph
A Writer's Notebook: Unlocking the Writing Within You (New and Expanded Addition)
HarperCollins, 2023

Ralph Fletcher has revised and expanded this foundational book, which has helped writers unlock their inner writers. In this new edition, Fletcher has included nine more chapters to build upon the wisdom shared for over twenty years, including new mentor texts, using photos to tell stories, and more. With humor, love, and wit, Fletcher offers more stories, strategies, and tips for documenting and recording our thoughts, ideas, and snippets of conversation—to gather for our writing.

Flor Ada, Alma, and Isabel Campoy
Authors in the Classroom: A Transformative Education Process
Pearson, 2003

In this book, Alma Flor Ada and Isabel Campoy advance an asset-based pedagogy that forges relationships among teachers, students, and families to cultivate literacy environments for authoring individual and collective selves. Using examples from teaching and professional development in diverse linguistic educational settings, they provide theoretical and evidence-based examples for writing instruction. The first chapters of the book stress theoretical foundations based on Paulo Freire's literacy framework, and the second part of the book provides ten practical units aligned with this freedom for liberation framework.

Graves, Donald H.
Newkirk, Thomas, and Penny Kittle (Eds).
Children Want to Write: Donald Graves and the Revolution in Children's Writing
Heinemann, 2013

Donald Graves's groundbreaking research changed writing instruction in classrooms across the country. Through careful, close, and intentional observation of young children at work, Graves documented children's composing processes, illuminating the importance of writing for authentic purposes. In this edited collection, Thomas Newkirk and Penny Kittle curated a collection of writings by Graves and videos from his research that transformed the ways that we see children and teach writers. In his writing and work alongside children and teachers, he offers a clear vision for creating learning environments that honor the voices and work of both children and teachers alike.

Heard, Georgia
Heart Maps: Helping Students Create and Craft Authentic Writing
Heinemann, 2016

Poet Georgia Heard first introduced us to the concept of heart maps in her book, *Awakening the Heart: Exploring Poetry in Elementary and Middle School*. Heart maps are a tool and strategy to inspire writers to write from the heart about what matters to them. In this book, Heard provides more ways (over twenty) that heart maps can be used in the writing classroom and beyond. Some templates and ideas that she includes are people we admire, wishes, gratitude, and so much more.

La Rocca, Whitney, and Jeff Anderson
Patterns of Wonder: Inviting Emergent Writers to Play with the Conventions of Language, PreK-1.
Stenhouse Publishers, 2022

Spotlighting curiosity and joy, play and talk in spaces such as reading, writing, and dramatic play centers, the authors center emerging innovative writing and reading skills of three- to six year olds. In a conversational format and based on rich classroom observations, the authors describe ways of instruction that can inspire young writers. The "patterns of wonder" process embraces engaging, playing, languaging, conferencing, celebrating, and grammar as everyday practices for composing stories in early childhood classrooms. The descriptions of dynamic and recursive phases of emergent writing provide a rich foundation for buzzing (turn and talk) in the preparation of early childhood teachers.

Laman, Tasha T.
From Ideas to Words: Writing Strategies for English Language Learners
Heinemann, 2013

From teaching in a diverse set of geographical spaces, the author offers samples of children's writing when they do not yet speak English. The author shows through illustrated classroom vignettes how teachers can engage students labeled as English language learners in the writing process and support their learning. Ways of planning lessons with meaningful and relevant content, building on background knowledge, and writing for authentic purposes are some of the principles highlighted in the book.

López-Robertson, Julia
Celebrating Our Cuentos: Choosing and Using Latinx Literature in Elementary Classrooms
Scholastic, 2021

This book pinpoints ways in which classrooms benefit from the inclusion of Latinx authors and illustrators for reading and writing lessons. The premise is that by giving students opportunities to see themselves, to see others, and to step into the world of others like and unlike themselves, authenticity is better understood. The teacher's ability to identify quality Latinx children's literature requires checking for bias, stereotypes, historical inclusion and exclusion, and more. Teachers and teacher educators will appreciate the books described and the pedagogical suggestions contained within its pages, including ways to promote family engagement with their children's literary experiences. The cultural appropriateness of themes and characters, as well as the social justice issues bound in the stories, are intentionally discussed.

Serravallo, Jennifer
Writing Strategies Book: Your Everything Guide to Developing Skilled Writers
Heinemann, 2017

Reviews claim that teachers can find treasures in this book because the clear organization of chapters showcase three-hundred strategies that work with struggling writers as well as gifted writers. For examples, teachers and future teachers can learn how to find a daily strategy based on grade levels, genre, or phases/stages of the writing process. Prompts, mentor text suggestions, language, and teaching tips for specific lessons are also included. Teachers also appreciate the appendix, which is filled with ideas for celebrating writing.

Online Resources

Colorincolorado.org

A bilingual language and literacy resource site for educators and families of English language learners in grades PreK–12, Colorín Colorado offers multimedia activities, videos, instructional tip sheets, featured author and illustrator videos, research-based articles, and resources to create an inclusive classroom environment and school community for all learners and their families. The website is bilingual in English and Spanish and offers parent content in thirteen languages, including Vietnamese, Chinese, Korean, Arabic, and Hmong.

Commonsense.org (education)

This site offers resources to navigate technology in an increasingly more tech-rich world. It provides a variety of lessons for teachers to integrate into their daily teaching, including videos, activities, and mini-lessons. This platform provides resources in English and Spanish.

Learningforjustice.org

Formerly Teaching Tolerance, Learning for Justice "seeks to uphold the mission of the Southern Poverty Law Center: to be catalyst for racial justice in the South and beyond, working in partnership with communities to dismantle white supremacy, strengthen intersectional movements, and advancement human rights for all people." It provides free educational resources focused on culture and climate, curriculum and instruction, leadership, and family and community engagement. Resources are digital and print-based, and offer interdisciplinary entry points into language, literacy, and civics teaching and learning.

Nationalgeographic.org

National Geographic is committed to teaching kids about the world to empower them to make it a better place. The site offers professional development, resources for the classroom, and special program experiences for students to engage with scientists and solve real-world issues.

Newsela.com

This site offers instructional materials to support student engagement with current events and historic and contemporary social justice issues. Content is aligned to teaching standards and available at different reading levels to support student learning across different grades.

Readwritethink.org

An online community for K–12 English language arts teachers, this platform provides resources including lesson plans, videos, booklists, and more to support the reading and writing development of students in and outside of school spaces.

Readworks.org

This site offers free print and digital reading and writing resources for K–12 teachers. There are paired texts on different topics, readings at differentiated levels, and videos. Additionally, this platform provides a ten-minute article-of-the-day readings.

Zinnproject.org

The Zinn Education Project promotes a true, accurate, and complex teaching of history. It offers resources to support teachers and teacher educators in teaching history beyond the textbook, engaging complex histories, sociopolitical contexts, and contemporary issues. The project provides teaching guides, readings, films, and more to support an in-depth and honest teaching of history.

References

Adichie, C. (2009). The danger of a single story. TED Talk, July 2009. Retrieved from www.ted.com/talks/chimamanda_adichie_the_danger_of_a_single_story.html

Alvarez, A. (2020). Experiential knowledge as capital and resistance among families from Mexican immigrant backgrounds. *Equity & Excellence in Education, 53*(4), 483–504. https://doi.org/10. 1080/10665684.2020.1791766

Alvarez, S. (2017). *Community literacies en confianza: Learning from bilingual after-school programs*. National Council of Teachers of English.

Anderson, J. (2019). Let's put conferring at the center of writing instruction. *Voices from the Middle, 26*(2), 9–13.

Anzaldúa, G. (1999). *Borderlands/la frontera: The new mestiza* (2nd ed.). Aunt Lute.

Bishop, R. S. (1990). Mirrors, windows, and sliding glass doors. *Perspectives, 6*(3), ix–xi.

Bomer, K. (2010). *Hidden gems: Naming and teaching from the brilliance in every student's writing*. Heinemann.

Calkins, L. M. (1994). *The art of teaching writing*. Heinemann.

Chapman, T. K. (2006). Interrogating classroom relationships and events: Using portraiture and critical race theory in education research. *Educational Researcher, 36*(3), 136–162.

Colato Laínez, R. (2005). *I am René, the boy*. Arte Público Press.

Colato Laínez, R. (2009). *René has two last names/ René tiene dos apellidos*. Arte Público Press.

Compton-Lilly, L. & Halverson, E. (2014). *Time and space in literacy research*. Routledge.

Darder, A. (1991). *Culture and power in the classroom*. Bergin & Garvey.

Darder, A. (2012). *Culture and power in the classroom* (2nd edition). Paradigm.

Di Pardo, A., Storms, B. A. & Selland, M. (2011). Seeing Voices: Assessing writerly stance in the NWP Analytic Writing Curriculum. *Assessing Writing, 16*(3), 170–188.

Dorfman, L. R., Cappelli, R. & Hoyt, L. (2017). *Mentor texts: Teaching writing through children's literature, K–6*. Stenhouse.

Dworin, J. E. (2006). The family stories project: Using funds of knowledge for writing. *The Reading Teacher, 59*(6), 510–520.

Dutro, E. & Haberl, E. (2018). Blurring material and rhetorical walls: Children writing the border/lands in a second-grade classroom. *Journal of Literacy Research, 50*(2), 167–189.

Dyson, A. H. (2020). "This isn't my real writing": The fate of children's agency in too-tight curricula. *Theory Into Practice, 59*(2), 119–127.

Ek, L. D., et al. (2013). Linguistic violence, insecurity, and work: Language ideologies of Latina/o bilingual teacher candidates in Texas. *International Multilingual Research Journal, 7*(3), 197–219.

Espinosa, C., M. & Ascenzi-Moreno, L. (2021). *Rooted in strength: Using translanguaging to grow multilingual readers and writers*. Scholastic.

Fletcher, R. (2013). *What a writer needs* (2nd ed.). Heinemann.

Fletcher, R. & Portalupi, J. (2001). *Writing workshop: The essential guide*. Heinemann.

Flint, A. & Rodriguez, S. (2013). Intentional moves to build community in the writer's workshop. In R.J. Meyer and K.F. Whitmore (Eds.) *Reclaiming writing: Composing spaces for identities, relationships and actions*, 168–178. Routledge.

Flores, T.T. (2023). "We are more than that!": Latina girls themselves from margins to center. *Research in the Teaching of English, 57*(4), 332–354.

Flores, T. T. (2021). Fighting to be heard: Latina adolescent girls writing toward change. *Journal of Adolescent & Adult Literacy, 65*(1), 65–73.

Flores, T. T. (2019). The family writing workshop: Latinx families cultivando comunidad through stories. *Language Arts, 97*(2), 59–71.

Flores, T. T., & Springer, S. (2021). Our legends and journey stories: Exploring culturally sustaining family engagement in classrooms. *Theory Into Practice, 60*(3), 312–321.

Fránquiz, M. E. and Salinas, C.S. (2022). Latinx teachers: Pláticas and possibilities. In C. D. Gist & T. J. Bristol (Eds.) *AERA Handbook of Research on Teachers of Color and Indigenous Teachers,* Chapter 31, pp. 417–429.

Fránquiz, M. E. & Del Carmen, S. M. (2004). The transformative potential of humanizing pedagogy: Addressing the diverse needs of Chicano/Mexicano students. *The High School Journal, 87*(4), 36–53. doi:10.1353/hsj.2004.0010

Fránquiz, M., Salazar, M. & DeNicolo, C. (2012). Challenging majoritarian tales: Portraits of bilingual teachers deconstructing deficit views. *Bilingual Research Journal, 34,* 279–300. doi: 10.1080/15235882.2011.625884

Fránquiz, M. E., et al. (2015). Figuring' bidirectional home and school connections along the biliteracy continuum. *Bilingual Research Journal, 38*(2), 152–171.

Freeman, D. E. & Freeman, Y. S. (2006). *Teaching reading and writing in Spanish and English in bilingual and dual language classrooms, Second edition.* Heinemann.

Freire, P. (1970). *Pedagogy of the oppressed.* New York, NY: Continuum Press.

García, E.E., Lawton, K. & Diniz de Figueiredo, E.H. (2012). The education of English language learners in Arizona: A history of underachievement. *Teachers College Record, 114*(9), 1–18.

Garcia, O. & Kleifgen, J.A. (2010). *Educating emergent bilinguals: Policies, programs, and practices for English language learners.* Teachers College Press.

Garcia, O., Kleifgen, J., & Falchi, L. (2008). From English language learners to emergent bilinguals. *Equity Matters: Research Review No. 1.* Teachers College, Columbia University.

García, O., Johnson, S. I. & Seltzer, K. (2017). *The translanguaging classroom: Leveraging student bilingualism for learning.* Caslon.

Gee, J.P. (2012). *Social linguistics and literacies: Ideology in discourse* (4th ed.). Routledge.

Gallo, S. (2017). *Mi padre: Mexican immigrant fathers and their children's education.* Teachers College Press.

Ghiso, M. P. (2011). "Writing that matters": Collaborative inquiry and authoring practices in a first-grade class. *Language Arts, 88*(5), 346–355.

González, N., Moll, L. C. & Amanti, C. (Eds.). (2005). *Funds of knowledge: Theorizing practices in households, communities, and classrooms.* Routledge.

Graves, D. (1983/2003). *Writing: Teachers and children at work.* Heinemann.

Gutiérrez, K. D., Morales, P. Z. & Martinez, D. C. (2009). Re-mediating literacy: Culture, difference, and learning for students from nondominant communities. *Review of Research in Education, 33*(1), 212–245.

Hawkins, L. K. (2016). The power of purposeful talk in the primary-grade writing conference. *Language Arts, 94*(1), 8–21.

Johnson, N. B. (1980). The material culture of public school classrooms: The symbolic integration of local schools and national culture. *Anthropology & Education Quarterly, 11*(3), 173–190.

Johnson, N. J., Koss, M. D. & Martinez, M. (2018). Through the sliding glass door: #EmpowerTheReader. *The Reading Teacher, 71*(5), 569–577.

Laman, T. T. (2014). Transforming literate identities: Writing and multilingual children at work. *Talking Points, 26*(1), 2–10.

Lawrence-Lightfoot, S. (2005). Reflections on portraiture: A dialogue between art and science. *Qualitative Inquiry, 11*(1), 3-15.

Lawrence-Lightfoot S. & Davis, J. H. (1997). *The art and science of portraiture.* Jossey Bass Publishers.

Leija, M. G. & Fránquiz, M. E. (2021). Building bridges between school and home: Teacher, parents, and students examining Latinx immigrant experiences. In G. Onchwari & S. Keengwe (Eds.) *Bridging Family-Teacher Relationships for ELL and Immigrant Students,* pp. 100–121. IGI Global Publishers.

Levy, J. (1995). *The spirit of Tío Fernando: A day of the dead story/Una historia del Día de Los Muertos.* Albert Whitman & Company.

Lewison, M. & Heffernan, L. (2008). Rewriting writers workshop: Creating safe spaces for disruptive stories. *Research in the Teaching of English 42*(4), 435–465.

Lillie, K. E., Markos, A., Arias, M. B. & Wiley, T. G. (2012). Separate and not equal: The implementation of structured English immersion in Arizona's classrooms. *Teachers College Record, 114*(9), 1–33.

López-Robertson, J. (2017). Diciendo cuentos/ Telling stories: Learning from and about the community cultural wealth of Latina Mamás through Latino children's literature. *Language Arts,* 95(1), 7–16.

López-Robertson, J. (2021). *Celebrating our cuentos: Choosing and using Latinx literature in elementary classrooms.* Scholastic.

López-Robertson, J. & Haney, M. J. (2016). Making it happen: Risk-taking and relevance in a rural elementary school. *Courageous leadership in early childhood education: Taking a stand for social justice,* 102–112.

López, M. M., Ynostroza, A., Fránquiz, M. E. & Curiel, L. C. (2015). Cultural artifacts: Using Sylvia and Aki for opening up authoring spaces. *Bilingual Research Journal, 38*(2), 190–206.

Moll, L. C., et al. (1992). Funds of knowledge for teaching: Using a qualitative approach to connect homes and classrooms. *Theory Into Practice, 31*(2), 132–141.

Morales, Y. (2016). *Just a minute: A trickster tale and counting Book.* Chronicle Books.

Moses, L., Serafini, F. & Loyd, S. (2016). Looking closely at informational texts: Considering the role(s) of mentor texts for kindergarten children. *Journal of Research in Childhood Education,* 30(4), 529–539.

Murray, R. (2015). *Writing in social spaces: A Social processes approach to academic writing.* Routledge Taylor & Francis Group.

Newman, B.M. (2012). Mentor texts and funds of knowledge: Situating writing within our students' worlds. *Voices from the Middle,* 20(1), 25–30.

Owocki, G. & Goodman, Y. (2002). *Kidwatching: Documenting children's literacy development.* Heinemann.

Paris, D. (2012). Culturally sustaining pedagogy: A needed change in stance, terminology, and practice. *Educational Researcher, 41*(3), 93–97.

Pérez, S. Z. (2002). Auto/ethnography and the politics of recovery: narrative anxiety in the borderlands of culture. *Recovering the US Hispanic Literary Heritage.* Eds. Jose Aranda Jr. and Silvio Torres-Saillant, *4,* 277–290.

Peterson, R. (1992). *Life in a crowded place: Making a learning community.* Heinemann.

Piña, P., Nash, K. T., Boardman, A., Polson, B. & Panther, L. (2015). Engaging children and families in culturally relevant literacies. *Journal of Family Strengths,* 1–26.

Ray, K.W. (1999). *Wondrous words: Writers and writing in the elementary classroom.* National Council of Teachers of English.

Reese, L. (2012). Storytelling in Mexican homes: Connections between oral and literacy practices. *Bilingual Research Journal, 35*(3), 277–293.

Rief, L. (2018). *The quickwrite handbook: 100 mentor texts to jumpstart your students' thinking and writing.* Heinemann.

Rief, L. (2002). Quickwrites: Leads to literacy. *Voices from the Middle, 10*(1), 50–51.

Rogoff, B. (1990). *Apprenticeship in thinking: Cognitive development in social context.* Oxford University.

Rumbaut, R. G. (2005) Sites of belonging: Acculturation, discrimination, and ethnic identity among children of immigrants. In T. S. Weisner (Ed.), *Discovering successful pathways in children's development: Mixed methods in the study of childhood and family life,* 111–162. University of Chicago Press.

Serafini, F. (2011). Creating space for children's literature. *The Reading Teacher, 65*(1), 30–34.

Serravallo, J. (2017). *The writing strategies book: Your everything guide to developing skilled writers.* Heinemann.

Sinclair, K. (2019). Disrupting normalized discourses: Ways of knowing, being and doing cultural competence. *The Australian Journal of Indigenous Education,* 1–9.

Street, B. (1995). *Social literacies: Critical approaches to literacy in development, ethnography, and education.* Longman.

Tellez, K. (1998). Class placement of elementary school emerging bilingual students. *Bilingual Research Journal, 22*(2-4), 279–295.

Tonatiuh, D. (2016). *Esquivel! Space-age sound artist.* Charlesbridge.

Tonatiuh, D. (2015). *Funny bones: Posada and his day of the dead calaveras.* Harry N. Abrams.

Tonatiuh, D. (2014). *Separate is never equal: Sylvia Mendez and her family's fight for desegregation.* Harry N. Abrams.

Tonatiuh, D. (2013). *Pancho Rabbit and the Coyote: A Migrant's Tale.* Harry N. Abrams.

Tonatiuh, D. (2010). *Dear Primo: A letter to my cousin.* Harry N. Abrams.

Villenas, S. (2001). Latina mothers and small-town racisms: Creating narratives of dignity and moral education in North Carolina. *Anthropology and Education Quarterly, 32*(1), 3–28.

Vygotsky, L. S. (1987). *Thought and language.* Cambridge, MA: MIT Press.

Wei, L. (2011). Moment analysis and trans-languaging space: Discursive construction of identities by multilingual Chinese youth in Britain. *Journal of Pragmatics, 43,* 1222–1235.

Wertsch, J. V. (1998). *Mind as action.* Oxford University Press.

Winn, M. T. & Johnson, L. P. (2011). *Writing instruction in the culturally relevant classroom.* National Council of Teachers of English.

Wohlwend, K. E. (2009). Dilemmas and discourses of learning to write: Assessment as a contested site. *Language Arts, 86*(5), 341–351.

Yosso, T. J. (2005). Whose culture has capital? A critical race theory discussion of community cultural wealth. *Race Ethnicity and Education, 8*(1), 69–91.

Children's and Young Adult Literature Cited

Alexander, K. (2014). *The crossover.* Houghton Mifflin Books.

Alexander, K., et al. (2017). *Out of wonder: Poems celebrating poets.* Candlewick Press.

Alvarez, J. (2005). *A gift of gracias: The legend of Altagracia.* Knopf Books for Young Readers.

Ancona, G. (1993). *Pablo remembers the fiesta of the day of the dead.* First Edition. New York, NY: HarperCollins.

Cervantes, J. (2014). *Tortilla sun.* Chronicle Books, LLC.

Colato Lainez, R. (2019). *My shoes and I: Crossing three borders/Mis zapatos y yo: Cruzando tres fronteras.* Arte Publico Piñata Books.

Coles, R. (1995). *The story of Ruby Bridges.* Scholastic.

Collins, S. (2014) *Mockingjay.* Scholastic.

Cordova, A. (2008). *Abuelita's heart.* Simon & Schuster Books.

Cornwall, G. (2017). *Jabari jumps.* Candlewick.

Dashner, J. (2010). *The maze runner.* Delacorte Press, Random House Children's Books.

Frame, J. A. (2008). *Yesterday I had the blues.* Tricycle Press, Ten Speed Press.

Garza, C. L. (2001). *In my family/En mi familia (Family pictures).* Children's Book Press.

Garza, Z. (2018) *Just one itsy bitsy little bite/ Sólo una mordidita chiquitita.* Houston, Texas. Piñata Books, Arte Público Press.

Haddix, M. P. (2000). *Among the hidden.* Simon & Schuster Books.

Herrera, J. P. (2006). *The upside down boy.* Children's Book Press.

Joseph, L. (2000). *The color of my words.* HarperCollins Children's Books.

Look, L. (1999). *Love as strong as ginger.* Atheneum Books for Young Readers.

Medina, M. (2018). *Merci Suárez changes gears.* Candlewick Press.

Morales, Y. (2018). *Dreamers.* Neil Porter Books.

Quintero, I. (2019). *My Papi has a motorcycle.* Kokila.

Reynolds, J. (2017). *Ghost.* Atheneum Books for Young Readers.

Ryan, M. (2012). *The dreamer.* Scholastic.

Rylant, C. (1982). *When I was young in the mountains.* Puffin Books, Penguin Putnam Books for Young Readers.

Say, A. (2008). *Grandfather's journey.* Houghton Mifflin.

Sotomayor, S. (2018). *Turning pages: My life story.* Philomel Books, Penguin Random House LLC.

Velasquez, E. (2004). *Grandma's records.* Bloomsbury USA Childrens.

Winter, J. (2019). *Our house is on fire: Greta Thurnberg's call to save the planet.* Beach Lane Books.

Woodson, J. (2018). *Harbor me.* Nancy Paulsen Books, Penguin Random House, LLC.

Index

Authors

Tracey T. Flores is an associate professor of language and literacy at the University of Texas at Austin. Flores is a former English language development (ELD) and English language arts (ELA) teacher, working for eight years alongside culturally and linguistically diverse students, families, and communities in K–8 schools throughout Glendale and Phoenix, Arizona. Her research focuses on Latina mothers' and daughters' language and literacy practices, the teaching of young writers in culturally and linguistically diverse classrooms, and family and community literacies. Flores is the founder of Somos Escritoras/We Are Writers, a writing and art workshop for Latina girls (grades 6–12) that invites them to share and perform stories from their lived experiences using art, theater, and writing as a tool for reflection, examination, and critique of their worlds. In addition, Flores is the co-chair of the Latinx Caucus of the National Council of Teachers of English (NCTE). She is a member of the 2016–2018 Cultivating New Voices Among Scholars of Color (CNV) cohort and Cohort Three of Professional Dyads and Culturally Responsive Teaching (PDCRT). Recently, she was named the 2019 Promising Researcher by the NCTE Standing Committee on Research.

María E. Fránquiz is a professor in the Department of Curriculum and Instruction at the University of Texas at Austin. She is an internationally recognized language and literacy scholar with thirty-plus years' experience as a teacher, teacher-educator, researcher, and administrator. Fránquiz has worked with students of every grade level in diverse geographic areas such as California, Alaska, Colorado, Utah, and Texas. She has coedited two books, *Inside the Latin@ Experience: A Latin@ Studies Reader* and *Scholars in the Field: The Challenges of Migrant Education*. Other publications include numerous peer-reviewed articles in professional journals, academic handbooks, edited books, and special topics journals. Among her professional service contributions are trustee of the NCTE Research Foundation, mentor and director of Cultivating New Voices Among Scholars of Color, and 2022–2023 NCTE president.

This book was typeset in Adobe Caslon Pro and PT Serif by Barbara Frazier.

Typefaces used on the cover include Chronicle Display, Avenir Next Medium, Avenir LT Com 65 Medium, and Avenir Book.

The book was printed on 50-lb., white, offset paper.